FIRM FOUNDATIONS

FIRM FOUNDATIONS

Knowing What You Believe

Dr. Stuart Pattico

SUNESIS MINISTRIES LTD

Firm Foundations: Knowing What You Believe

ISBN 978-0-9930065-8-6

Published by Sunesis Ministries Ltd. For more information about Sunesis Ministries Ltd, please visit:

www.stuartpattico.com

Scripture quotations marked NKJV are from the Holy Bible, New King James Version Copyright © 1982 Thomas Nelson, Inc. Used by permission. All rights reserved. Scripture quotations marked ESV are taken from The Holy Bible, English Standard Version Copyright © 2001 by Crossway Bibles, a division of Good News Publishers. Scripture quotations marked KJV are from the Holy Bible, King James Version. Scripture quotations marked NLT are taken from the Holy Bible, New Living Translation, copyright © 1996, 2004, 2007 by Tyndale House Foundation. Used by permission of Tyndale House Publishers, Inc., Carol Stream, Illinois 60188. All rights reserved.
Scripture quotations marked NRSV are from the New Revised Standard Version Bible, copyright © 1989 the Division of Christian Education of the National Council of the Churches of Christ in the United States of America. Used by permission. All rights reserved. Scripture quotations marked KJV are from the Holy Bible, King James Version. Scripture quotations marked YLT are from the Holy Bible, Young's Literal Translation. Scripture quotations marked "Amplified" are taken from the Amplified Bible, copyright © 2015 by The Lockman Foundation, La Habra, CA 90631. All rights reserved. For Permission To Quote information visit http://www.lockman.org/
The "Amplified" trademark is registered in the United States Patent and Trademark Office by The Lockman Foundation. Use of this trademark requires the permission of The Lockman Foundation. Scripture quotations marked HCSB are taken from the Holman Christian Standard Bible®, Copyright © 1999, 2000, 2002, 2003, 2009 by Holman Bible Publishers. Used by permission. Holman Christian Standard Bible®, Holman CSB®, and HCSB® are federally registered trademarks of Holman Bible Publishers. Quotations marked NEB are from The New English Bible: The New Testament © 'The Delegates of the Oxford University Press and the Syndics of the Cambridge University Press 1961, 1970.

Wherever a part of a quotation is bold or underlined, this emphasis has been added by the author, and is not bold or underlined in the original quotation. Also, when any part of a quotation is in [square brackets], this has been added by the author for clarification, and is not part of the original quotation, except when quoting from the Amplified Bible.

The author of this book does not dispense medical advice or prescribe the use of any technique as a form of treatment for physical, emotional, or medical problems without the advice of a physician, either directly or indirectly. The intent of the author is only to offer information of a general nature to help you in your quest for emotional and spiritual well-being. In the event you use any of the information in this book for yourself, the author and publisher assume no responsibility for your actions.

Contents

Introduction

I initially wrote this book as a training course for members of the church I pastor. It is my prayer that it will be a blessing to the wider body of Christ also.

It is my observation that most people's spiritual struggles are not due to a failure to grasp some advanced area of theology. It is usually due to a crack in the foundation. However, having a firm and clear grasp of the foundational truths of Scripture will enable you to be victorious in your Christian journey.

In this book, I cover fifteen key areas, namely, what we believe about: God, Jesus Christ, the Holy Spirit, Humanity, Salvation, Grace vs. Law, the Church, the Baptism in the Holy Spirit, Healing, Angels & Heavenly Beings, the Enemy, Prayer, Worship, Death, and the Second Coming of Jesus Christ.

This resource can be used by new and mature believers alike. It is also useful as a teaching aid for pastors and ministers to use in Bible studies. The writing style in this book is intentionally simple and to the point, so that it is both accessible and able to also be used as a teaching aid.

This book contains my personal understanding of the matters addressed, and so readers are always encouraged to check these things out for themselves and to do their own research.

Shalom,

Dr. Stuart Pattico
Senior Pastor, Joy Community Church

1

God

In this chapter, we will look at some of the basic biblical truths about who God is.

God created all things:

> Genesis 1:1 (NKJV)
> In the beginning God created the heavens and the earth.

God is Himself uncreated:

> Psalm 90:2 (NKJV)
> ² Before the mountains were brought forth,
> Or ever You had formed the earth and the world,
> Even from everlasting to everlasting, You *are* God.

God has a name. In Hebrew it is "YHWH", which is usually translated "the LORD" (with block capitals) in the Old Testament.

Psalm 83:18 (NKJV)
[18] That they may know that You, whose name alone
is the Lord [YHWH],
Are the Most High over all the earth.

We do not know how YHWH was pronounced, but "Yahweh" is a popular suggestion. The New Testament writers didn't insist that Christians attempt to pronounce YHWH, but were happy to use the Greek equivalent of "Lord" when quoting from the Old Testament:

The name YHWH means "He always is". There are various other titles connected to the name "YHWH" in the Old Testament:

Name	Meaning
YHWH Yireh (Genesis 22:14)	The LORD will provide
YHWH Ropheka (Exodus 15:26)	The LORD your healer
YHWH Nissi (Exodus 17:15)	The LORD is my banner (victory)
YHWH Mekoddishkem (Exodus 31:13)	The LORD your sanctifier
YHWH Shalom (Judges 6:24)	The LORD is peace
YHWH Rohi (Psalm 23:1)	The LORD is my shepherd
YHWH Tsidkenu (Jeremiah 23:6)	The LORD is our righteousness
YHWH Shammah (Ezekiel 48:35)	The LORD is there

God is omnipotent i.e. He can do anything He wants to do:

Luke 1:37 (NKJV)
[37] For with God nothing will be impossible.

God is omnipresent i.e. He is everywhere:

Psalm 139:7 (NKJV)
[7] Where can I go from Your Spirit?
Or where can I flee from Your presence?

God is omniscient i.e. He knows everything:

Proverbs 15:3 (NKJV)
[3] The eyes of the LORD *are* in every place,
Keeping watch on the evil and the good.

God is holy. The word "holy" means "set apart". God is set apart from sin, and also set apart in the sense that He is unique – there is no one like Him:

Isaiah 6:3 (NKJV)
[3] "Holy, holy, holy *is* the LORD of hosts;
The whole earth *is* full of His glory!"

God is invisible:

1 Timothy 1:17 (NKJV)
[17] Now to the King eternal, immortal, invisible, to God who alone is wise, *be* honor and glory forever and ever. Amen.

God is immaterial (spirit). Science can never discover God, He discloses Himself by revelation:

John 4:24 (ESV)
24 God is spirit, and those who worship him must worship in spirit and truth."

God is eternal. This means that He will never cease to exist:

Psalm 90:2 (NKJV)
² Even from everlasting to everlasting, You *are* God.

God is good:

Psalm 34:8 (NKJV)
⁸ Oh, taste and see that the LORD *is* good;

God is righteous. He can only do what is right:

Ezra 9:15 (NKJV)
¹⁵ O LORD God of Israel, You *are* righteous...

God is light; there is no evil to be found in Him:

1 John 1:5 (NKJV)
⁵ ... God is light and in Him is no darkness at all.

God is a consuming fire – He is not to be messed with:

Hebrews 12:29 (NKJV)
²⁹ For our God *is* a consuming fire.

God is wise:

Jude 25 (NKJV)
[25] To God our Savior,
Who alone is wise,
Be glory and majesty,
Dominion and power,
Both now and forever.
Amen.

God is love:

1 John 4:16 (NKJV)
[16] … God is love…

God is one. There is only one true God.

Deuteronomy 6:4 (NKJV)
[4] "Hear, O Israel: The LORD our God, the LORD *is* one!

2

Jesus Christ

In this chapter, we will turn our attention to God's Son, Jesus Christ:

> Mark 1:1 (NKJV)
> The beginning of the gospel of Jesus Christ, the Son of God.

Jesus has always existed:

> Colossians 1:17 (NKJV)
> [17] And He [Jesus] is before all things, and in Him all things consist.

> Revelation 22:13 (NKJV)
> [13] I [Jesus] am the Alpha and the Omega, *the* Beginning and *the* End, the First and the Last."

Jesus is the one through whom God created all things:

Ephesians 3:9 (NKJV)
⁹ ... God who created all things through Jesus Christ;

John 1:3 (NKJV)
³ All things were made through Him [Jesus], and without Him nothing was made that was made.

Notice that "all things" were created through Jesus. This means that Jesus Himself is uncreated, as nothing "created" exists that was not created by Jesus. So where did Jesus come from? He has always derived His being from God His Father. This is described in the New Testament as Him being "begotten" of God. It is an eternal reality that has no beginning:

1 John 4:9 (NKJV)
⁹ In this the love of God was manifested toward us, that God has sent His only begotten Son into the world, that we might live through Him.

John 6:57 (NKJV)
⁵⁷ As the living Father sent Me, and I live because of the Father, so he who feeds on Me will live because of Me.

God and His Son Jesus communicate with each other. As far back as Genesis, the Bible records God speaking with His Son about the creation of mankind:

Genesis 1:26 (NKJV)
²⁶ Then God said, "Let Us make man in Our image, according to Our likeness; let them have dominion over the fish of the sea, over the birds of the air,

and over the cattle, over all the earth and over every creeping thing that creeps on the earth."

Who was God speaking to when He said "Us"? It must have been someone who shares His "image", since He said "Let Us make man in **Our image**". That person is Jesus Christ His Son. Because Jesus is just like His Father, He is called "the image of God":

> 2 Corinthians 4:4 (NKJV)
> [4] ... Christ, who is the image of God

> Colossians 1:15 (NKJV)
> [15] He is the image of the invisible God, the firstborn over all creation.

Jesus sustains the universe:

> Hebrews 1:3 (ESV)
> **3** ...he [Jesus] upholds the universe by the word of his power...

Jesus became a human being, and was born of the virgin Mary:

> Galatians 4:4 (NKJV)
> [4] But when the fullness of the time had come, God sent forth His Son, born of a woman, born under the law,

> Matthew 1:21 (NKJV)
> [21] And she will bring forth a Son, and you shall call His name JESUS, for He will save His people from their sins."

In His earthly ministry, Jesus healed the sick, taught, and preached about the kingdom of God. Although He was the eternal Son of God, He did not use His power as God's Son in His ministry. Instead, He acted as a human being completely dependent on the Holy Spirit's power:

> Matthew 4:23 (NKJV)
> [23] And Jesus went about all Galilee, teaching in their synagogues, preaching the gospel of the kingdom, and healing all kinds of sickness and all kinds of disease among the people.

> Acts 10:38 (NKJV)
> [38] how God anointed Jesus of Nazareth with the Holy Spirit and with power, who went about doing good and healing all who were oppressed by the devil, for God was with Him.

As a Man, Jesus never sinned:

> Hebrews 4:15 (NKJV)
> [15] For we do not have a High Priest who cannot sympathize with our weaknesses, but was in all *points* tempted as *we are, yet* without sin.

In His earthly ministry, and throughout eternity, Jesus has always worked in perfect unison with God the Father. So great is the unity they share, that Jesus referred to Himself and God as being "one" and explained this by saying that God is in Him and He is in God:

> John 10:30,38 (NKJV)
> [30] I and *My* Father are one... [38] the Father *is* in Me,

and I in Him.

As a Man, Jesus was crucified for our sins, and rose from the dead three days later. He ascended into heaven where He is now seated at the right hand of God:

> 1 Corinthians 15:3-4 (NKJV)
> ³ For I delivered to you first of all that which I also received: that Christ died for our sins according to the Scriptures, ⁴ and that He was buried, and that He rose again the third day according to the Scriptures,

> Mark 16:19 (NKJV)
> ¹⁹ So then, after the Lord had spoken to them, He was received up into heaven, and sat down at the right hand of God.

God has now made Jesus "Lord" and "Christ". "Lord" in this context means that He is the ruler of the universe, and "Christ" (which means "anointed one") indicates that God has anointed Him as King:

> Acts 2:36 (NKJV)
> ³⁶ "Therefore let all the house of Israel know assuredly that God has made this Jesus, whom you crucified, both Lord and Christ."

> 1 Corinthians 8:6 (NKJV)
> ⁶ yet for us *there is* one God, the Father, of whom *are* all things, and we for Him; and one Lord Jesus Christ, through whom *are* all things, and through whom we *live.*

Jesus is the Head of the church:

> Colossians 1:18 (NKJV)
> [18] And He is the head of the body, the church...

Jesus prays to God for the church:

> Romans 8:34 (NKJV)
> [34] Who *is* he who condemns? *It is* Christ who died, and furthermore is also risen, who is even at the right hand of God, who also makes intercession for us.

Although He is Lord, Jesus is subject to God His Father:

> 1 Corinthians 11:3 (NKJV)
> [3] But I want you to know that the head of every man is Christ, the head of woman *is* man, and the head of Christ *is* God.

Jesus is the only means by which humanity can be saved:

> Acts 4:12 (NKJV)
> [12] Nor is there salvation in any other, for there is no other name under heaven given among men by which we must be saved."

Jesus is called "the Word". This means that He is the perfect communication of who God is ("like Father, like Son"). Therefore, if we want to know what God is like, all we need to do is to look at Jesus:

> John 1:14 (NKJV)
> [14] And the Word [Jesus] became flesh and dwelt

among us, and we beheld His glory, the glory as of the only begotten of the Father, full of grace and truth.

John 14:9 (NKJV)
[9] ...He who has seen Me has seen the Father...

When a father begets a son, the son has the same human nature as his father. Because Jesus is God's Son, He has the same nature as His Father – God. Therefore, Jesus can also be referred to as "God". This reference means that Jesus' very nature is "God", even though He is a distinct person from Him:

John 1:1 (NKJV)
In the beginning was the Word [Jesus], and the Word was with God, and the Word was God.

In the clause, "the Word was God", the original Greek does not have a definite article before the word "God". In Greek grammar, a definite article is like our English word "the". It is similar to the gesture of someone pointing at something and saying "this one". When there is no definite article, it sometimes indicates that the word following is characteristic of the subject of that clause. For example, in 1 John 1:5 we read, "God is light". The original Greek has no definite article before "light", which indicates that "light" is characteristic of "God". In other words, "light" describes the nature of God. Even so, the absence of the definite article before "God" in the last clause of John 1:1 indicates that "God" is characteristic of "the Word". John is basically saying that the very nature of the Word is "God". He is saying that **the Word is everything that God is**. In light of the construction in the original Greek, the best translation of John 1:1 I have come across is found in the New English Bible. It reads as follows:

> John 1:1 (NEB)
> When all things began, the Word already was. The Word dwelt with God, and **what God was, the Word was**.

Here are two other verses in which Jesus is referred to as "God":

> John 20:28 (NKJV)
> [28] And Thomas answered and said to Him [Jesus], "My Lord and my God!"

> Philippians 2:5-6 (NIV)
> [5] In your relationships with one another, have the same mindset as Christ Jesus:
> [6] Who, being in very nature God, did not consider equality with God something to be used to his own advantage;

Likewise, the following verse also affirms the deity of Christ:

> Colossians 2:9 (ESV)
> [9] For in him [Jesus] the whole fullness of deity dwells bodily,

Because Jesus is "in very nature God", He is to be worshipped, just like God is worshipped:

John 5:23 (NKJV)
²³ that all should honor the Son just as they honor the Father. He who does not honor the Son does not honor the Father who sent Him.

Hebrews 1:6 (NKJV)
⁶ But when He again brings the firstborn into the world, He says:
"Let all the angels of God worship Him."

The Bible states, "there is one God" (1 Corinthians 8:6; 1 Timothy 2:5). If both God and Jesus are called "God", how can there be only "one God"? The solution becomes clear when we examine the statements that there is "one God" in their context:

1 Corinthians 8:6 (NKJV)
⁶ yet for us *there is* one God, the Father, of whom *are* all things, and we for Him; and one Lord Jesus Christ, through whom *are* all things, and through whom we *live.*

1 Timothy 2:5 (NKJV)
⁵ For *there is* one God and one Mediator between God and men, *the* Man Christ Jesus,

In these verses, it is quite clear that the phrase, "there is one God", is not a reference to Jesus, but is a reference to God the Father. In 1 Corinthians 8:6, there is "one God, the Father"; in 1 Timothy 2:5, Jesus is not identified as the "one God", but is instead identified as the one who mediates between the "one God" and men.

When the Bible states that there is only one God, it

doesn't mean that there is no one else who shares His very nature (i.e. His deity). Both the Son and the Holy Spirit (whom we will study in the next chapter) share God's nature. What it means is that there is only one person who is the source of Himself and subordinate to no one. That person is God the Father alone. Jesus is not His own source - He is begotten of the Father and is subordinate to Him:

> 1 John 4:9 (NKJV)
> [9] In this the love of God was manifested toward us, that God has sent His only begotten Son into the world, that we might live through Him.

> 1 Corinthians 11:3 (NKJV)
> [3] But I want you to know that the head of every man is Christ, the head of woman *is* man, and the head of Christ *is* God.

Therefore, in the sense that there is only one who has no source, we can say that there is only one God. However, there is a trinity of eternal persons who share His nature – Himself, His Son, and His Spirit.

As we have seen from numerous verses in this chapter, God and His Son Jesus are distinct persons. Unfortunately, some have misunderstood the following passage and wrongly interpreted it to mean that Jesus Christ is God the Father:

> Isaiah 9:6-7 (NKJV)
> [6] For unto us a Child is born,
> Unto us a Son is given;
> And the government will be upon His shoulder.

And His name will be called
Wonderful, Counselor, Mighty God,
Everlasting Father, Prince of Peace.
⁷ Of the increase of *His* government and peace
There will be no end,
Upon the throne of David and over His kingdom,
To order it and establish it with judgment and justice
From that time forward, even forever.
The zeal of the LORD of hosts will perform this.

One of the titles given to Jesus in this passage is "Everlasting Father". However, this does not mean that He is God the Father. The passage is a prophecy about the coming Messiah who would sit as king upon "the throne of David" (v7). In Mark 11:10, the crowd cried out, "Blessed is the kingdom of our father David". Notice, David was referred to as "our father". Like King David, Jesus will be a father to His people as He reigns over them as their king. However, unlike David who only reigned for 40 years, Jesus will reign *forever*. Therefore, He is called "*Everlasting* Father". As such, this title is a reference to Jesus' eternal kingly function as Messiah. It is not a reference to God the Father, who is clearly distinguished from His Son throughout the New Testament.

3

The Holy Spirit

We will now explore the person and work of the Holy Spirit.

In the last chapter, we explored the fact that God the Father has a Son called Jesus Christ. The Father loves the Son, and the Son loves the Father.

> John 5:20 (NKJV)
> [20] For the Father loves the Son, and shows Him all things that He Himself does; and He will show Him greater works than these, that you may marvel.

> John 14:31 (NKJV)
> [31] But that the world may know that I [Jesus] love the Father, and as the Father gave Me commandment, so I do. Arise, let us go from here.

But how do the Father and the Son express their love for each other? They do so through another person called the Holy Spirit. The Spirit emanates from God and His

Son Jesus as the expression of the love they share for each other. Throughout eternity, the Spirit has been relaying to the Father and the Son their mutual love. For example, when the Son wants to affectionately call God "Daddy", it is the Spirit emanating from Him that communicates this message to God:

> Galatians 4:6 (NKJV)
> [6] And because you are sons, God has sent forth the Spirit of His Son into your hearts, crying out, "Abba, Father!"

Paul's point in this verse is that the Spirit expresses the relational love the Son has for the Father in the cry, "Abba, Father!" ("Abba" means "Daddy"). Paul reasons that because the same Spirit lives in our heart, the same cry of "Abba, Father" is present within us so that through the Spirit we also can relate to God as Father, just as Jesus does.

Similarly, when the Father wishes to communicate His love for His Son, He does so by the Spirit. This is why, when Jesus was baptised, and God wanted to publicly announce how much He loved His Son, the Spirit visibly descended on Jesus in the form of a dove. This episode in time gave us a glimpse into what is constantly taking place in eternity – the Spirit emanating from God as the expression of His love for His Son:

> Luke 3:22 (NKJV)
> [22] And the Holy Spirit descended in bodily form like a dove upon Him, and a voice came from heaven which said, "You are My beloved Son; in You I am well pleased."

As the expression of the love that God has for His Son, the Spirit causes the Son to know how much the Father loves Him. Similarly, when the same Spirit enters our heart, He also expresses the love that God has for us:

> Romans 5:5 (NKJV)
> ⁵ Now hope does not disappoint, because the love of God has been poured out in our hearts by the Holy Spirit who was given to us.

In the last two chapters, we have seen that both God and His Son Jesus have always existed. Therefore, the love they share for each has always existed. As such, the Spirit, who is the expression of their love, has always existed also – He is eternal:

> Hebrews 9:14 (NKJV)
> ¹⁴ how much more shall the blood of Christ, who through the **eternal Spirit** offered Himself without spot to God, cleanse your conscience from dead works to serve the living God?

In the last chapter, we saw that Jesus is in very nature God because He is God's Son. Because the Spirit emanates from God and Jesus Christ, He too has the very nature of God, and can therefore be referred to as "God" in the sense that He is the emanation of God's nature. In the following passage, Peter uses the terms "the Holy Spirit" and "God" interchangeably:

> Acts 5:1–4 (NKJV)
> But a certain man named Ananias, with Sapphira his wife, sold a possession. ² And he kept back *part*

of the proceeds, his wife also being aware *of it,* and brought a certain part and laid *it* at the apostles' feet. ³But Peter said, "Ananias, why has Satan filled your heart to lie to **the Holy Spirit** and keep back *part* of the price of the land for yourself? ⁴While it remained, was it not your own? And after it was sold, was it not in your own control? Why have you conceived this thing in your heart? You have not lied to men but to **God**."

Because God, His Son Jesus, and the Holy Spirit all share the divine nature, Christians often refer to them collectively as the Trinity (i.e. tri-unity). There are various passages that mention all three persons of the Trinity. In the following quotations, each person of the Trinity is highlighted in bold:

Matthew 3:16–17 (NKJV)
¹⁶When He had been baptized, **Jesus** came up immediately from the water; and behold, the heavens were opened to Him, and He saw **the Spirit of God** descending like a dove and alighting upon Him. ¹⁷And suddenly **a voice *came* from heaven** [God the Father], saying, "This is My beloved Son, in whom I am well pleased."

Matthew 28:19 (NKJV)
¹⁹Go therefore and make disciples of all the nations, baptizing them in the name of **the Father** and of **the Son** and of **the Holy Spirit**,

John 15:26 (NKJV)
²⁶"But when the Helper comes, whom I shall send to you from **the Father**, **the Spirit of truth** who

proceeds from the Father, He will testify of **Me** [Jesus].

Acts 10:38 (NKJV)
[38] how **God** anointed **Jesus** of Nazareth with **the Holy Spirit** and with power, who went about doing good and healing all who were oppressed by the devil, for God was with Him.

2 Corinthians 13:14 (NKJV)
[14] The grace of **the Lord Jesus Christ**, and the love of **God**, and the communion of **the Holy Spirit** *be* with you all. Amen.

Romans 15:30 (NKJV)
[30] Now I beg you, brethren, through **the Lord Jesus Christ**, and through the love of **the Spirit**, that you strive together with me in prayers to **God** for me,

It is important to realise that the Spirit is Himself a *person* who expresses the mutual love of the Father and the Son, and not a mere impersonal conduit of that love. In order for their mutual love to be adequately expressed, it requires an actual person; an impersonal force could never perfectly express divine love. It is therefore important that we relate to the Holy Spirit as a person, and not merely as a force. That He is a person is evident from the fact that He speaks; and has a mind, will and emotions. The Holy Spirit is not an "it", the Spirit is a "He":

Acts 10:19 (NKJV)
[19] ... the Spirit **said** to him, "Behold, three men are seeking you.

Romans 8:27 (NKJV)
[27] Now He who searches the hearts knows what the **mind** of the Spirit *is...*

1 Corinthians 12:11 (NKJV)
[11] But one and the same Spirit works all these things, distributing to each one individually as **He wills**.

Isaiah 63:10 (NKJV)
[10] But they rebelled and **grieved** His Holy Spirit;

Here are some of the names by which the Holy Spirit is known:

- The Spirit of God (Genesis 1:2)
- The Spirit of YHWH (Judges 3:10)
- The Spirit of Wisdom and Understanding (Isaiah 11:2)
- The Spirit of Counsel and Might (Isaiah 11:2)
- The Spirit of Knowledge and of the Fear of Jehovah (Isaiah 11:2)
- The Spirit of the Lord YHWH (Isaiah 61:1)
- The Spirit of Grace and Supplication (Zechariah 12:10)
- The Spirit of your Father (Matthew 10:20)
- The Finger of God (Luke 11:20, compare Matthew 12:28)
- The Spirit of Holiness (Romans 1:4)
- The Spirit of Truth (John 14:17)
- The Helper / Comforter (John 14:26)
- The Spirit of the Lord (Acts 5:9)
- The Spirit of Jesus (Acts 16:6-7)
- The Spirit of Life (Romans 8:2)

- The Spirit of Christ (Romans 8:9)
- The Spirit of Adoption (Romans 8:15)
- The Spirit of the Living God (2 Corinthians 3:3)
- The Spirit (Galatians 5:16)
- The Holy Spirit of Promise (Ephesians 1:13)
- The Holy Spirit of God (Ephesians 4:30)
- The Spirit of Jesus Christ (Philippians 1:19)
- The Eternal Spirit (Hebrews 9:14)
- The Spirit of Grace (Hebrews 10:29)
- The Spirit of Glory (1 Peter 4:14)
- The Anointing (1 John 2:27)
- The Seven Spirits of God (Revelation 5:6, this name depicts the sevenfold anointing of the Spirit upon Jesus as described in Isaiah 11:1-2)

In addition to being the expression of love shared by God the Father and His Son, the Spirit is also the active power of God throughout the universe. This is evident by the fact that the Spirit is the means by which things are created. God created through His Son, by the power of the Spirit:

> Psalm 104:30 (NKJV)
> [30] You send forth Your Spirit, they are created;
> And You renew the face of the earth.

The Spirit is the means by which God is present everywhere in the universe:

> Psalm 139:7 (NKJV)
> [7] Where can I go from Your Spirit?
> Or where can I flee from Your presence?

The Spirit is the means by which God knows everything

that is happening everywhere. He is the metaphorical "eyes" of God:

> Proverbs 15:3 (NKJV)
> [3] The eyes of the LORD *are* in every place,
> Keeping watch on the evil and the good.

> Revelation 5:6 (NKJV)
> [6] And I looked, and behold, in the midst of the throne and of the four living creatures, and in the midst of the elders, stood a Lamb as though it had been slain, having seven horns and seven eyes, which are the seven Spirits of God sent out into all the earth.

The Spirit is the means through which God empowers His servants. The supreme example of this is the Spirit's empowerment of Jesus Christ when He became a human being. It was the Spirit who enabled Christ to work miracles:

> Acts 10:38 (NKJV)
> [38] how God anointed Jesus of Nazareth with the Holy Spirit and with power, who went about doing good and healing all who were oppressed by the devil, for God was with Him.

The Spirit also gives special abilities (i.e. spiritual gifts) to Christians so that they can serve God and one another:

> 1 Corinthians 12:7-11 (NKJV)
> [7] But the manifestation of the Spirit is given to each one for the profit *of all:* [8] for to one is given the word of wisdom through the Spirit, to another

the word of knowledge through the same Spirit, [9] to another faith by the same Spirit, to another gifts of healings by the same Spirit, [10] to another the working of miracles, to another prophecy, to another discerning of spirits, to another *different* kinds of tongues, to another the interpretation of tongues. [11] But one and the same Spirit works all these things, distributing to each one individually as He wills.

The Spirit was the supernatural means by which Jesus became a human being:

Matthew 1:18 (NKJV)
[18] Now the birth of Jesus Christ was as follows: After His mother Mary was betrothed to Joseph, before they came together, she was found with child of the Holy Spirit.

The Spirit is the means by which God lives in His children, enabling us to experientially know God as our Father:

Romans 8:15–16 (NKJV)
[15] For you did not receive the spirit of bondage again to fear, but you received the Spirit of adoption by whom we cry out, "Abba, Father." [16] The Spirit Himself bears witness with our spirit that we are children of God

The Spirit is the means by which God inspired the Bible. The biblical authors were led by the Spirit so that what they wrote is in fact the word of God. Therefore, for Christians, the Bible is the final authority on all matters of faith and conduct, and a vital way that we experience the Holy Spirit's ministry:

> 2 Timothy 3:16 (NKJV)
> [16] All Scripture *is* given by inspiration of God, and *is* profitable for doctrine, for reproof, for correction, for instruction in righteousness,

> 2 Peter 1:20-21 (NKJV)
> [20] knowing this first, that no prophecy of Scripture is of any private interpretation, [21] for prophecy never came by the will of man, but holy men of God spoke *as they were* moved by the Holy Spirit.

The Spirit is the means by which God enables people to understand His truth:

> John 16:13 (NKJV)
> [13] However, when He, the Spirit of truth, has come, He will guide you into all truth; for He will not speak on His own *authority,* but whatever He hears He will speak; and He will tell you things to come.

The Spirit empowers Christians to pray effectively:

> Jude 20 (NKJV)
> [20] But you, beloved, building yourselves up on your most holy faith, praying in the Holy Spirit,

The Spirit is the means by which Christians are marked as belonging to God:

> Ephesians 4:30 (NKJV)
> [30] And do not grieve the Holy Spirit of God, by

whom you were sealed for the day of redemption.

The Spirit is the means by which Christians have a foretaste of the coming age:

> Ephesians 1:14 (Amplified)
> [14] The Spirit is the guarantee [the first installment, the pledge, a foretaste] of our inheritance until the redemption of *God's own* [purchased] possession [His believers], to the praise of His glory.

The Spirit is the means by which we are made like Jesus:

> 2 Corinthians 3:18 (NKJV)
> [18] But we all, with unveiled face, beholding as in a mirror the glory of the Lord, are being transformed into the same image from glory to glory, just as by the Spirit of the Lord.

The Spirit is the power by which we can live godly lives:

> Galatians 5:16 (NKJV)
> [16] I say then: Walk in the Spirit, and you shall not fulfill the lust of the flesh.

> Galatians 5:22–23 (NKJV)
> [22] But the fruit of the Spirit is love, joy, peace, long-suffering, kindness, goodness, faithfulness, [23] gentleness, self-control. Against such there is no law.

Through the church, the Spirit convicts the world of sin, righteousness and of judgement:

John 16:8 (NKJV)
[8] And when He [the Spirit] has come, He will convict the world of sin, and of righteousness, and of judgment...

The Spirit guides Christians. For example, the Spirit's leading did not allow Paul and his team to enter Asia or Bithynia, but directed them instead to Macedonia:

Acts 16:6–10 (NKJV)
[6] Now when they had gone through Phrygia and the region of Galatia, they were forbidden by the Holy Spirit to preach the word in Asia. [7] After they had come to Mysia, they tried to go into Bithynia, but the Spirit did not permit them. [8] So passing by Mysia, they came down to Troas. [9] And a vision appeared to Paul in the night. A man of Macedonia stood and pleaded with him, saying, "Come over to Macedonia and help us." [10] Now after he had seen the vision, immediately we sought to go to Macedonia, concluding that the Lord had called us to preach the gospel to them.

The Spirit prays to God for Christians:

Romans 8:27 (NKJV)
[27] [the Spirit] makes intercession for the saints...

The Spirit empowers Christians to be a witness for Jesus Christ:

Acts 1:8 (NKJV)
[8] But you shall receive power when the Holy Spirit has come upon you; and you shall be witnesses to

Me in Jerusalem, and in all Judea and Samaria, and to the end of the earth."

In the Bible, there are various symbols that are used to represent the Holy Spirit, all of which help us to understand more about Him. Here are seven of them...

1. Fire – this represents the burning away of sin, blazing glory, and zeal for God that the Holy Spirit brings into our lives:

> Acts 2:3-4 (NKJV)
> [3] Then there appeared to them divided tongues, as of fire, and *one* sat upon each of them. [4] And they were all filled with the Holy Spirit and began to speak with other tongues, as the Spirit gave them utterance.

2. A dove - portrays the Holy Spirit as a person who is gentle and comforting:

> Luke 3:22 (NKJV)
> [22] And the Holy Spirit descended in bodily form like a dove upon Him, and a voice came from heaven which said, "You are My beloved Son; in You I am well pleased."

3. Water - denotes the fact that the Holy Spirit gives life and refreshment to those who receive Him. He satisfies our spiritual thirst:

> John 7:38-39 (NKJV)
> [38] He who believes in Me, as the Scripture has said, out of his heart will flow rivers of living water."

[39] But this He spoke concerning the Spirit, whom those believing in Him would receive; for the Holy Spirit was not yet *given,* because Jesus was not yet glorified.

4. Wind - in nature, wind is a powerful force, as is evident from the destruction that it can cause. Even so, the emblem of wind portrays the Holy Spirit as God's divine power:

> Acts 2:2 (NKJV)
> [2] And suddenly there came a sound from heaven, as of a rushing mighty wind, and it filled the whole house where they were sitting.

5. Oil - in the Old Testament, oil was used to consecrate selected persons for their service (e.g. Exodus 28:41). In the New Testament, we have the anointing of the Holy Spirit. The emblem of oil points to the fact that the Spirit consecrates and empowers us for service:

> 1 John 2:27 (NKJV)
> [27] But the anointing which you have received from Him abides in you...

6. A seal - in the days of the New Testament, a "seal" served as a stamp of ownership. The Holy Spirit's presence in our lives marks us as belonging to God:

> Ephesians 4:30 (NKJV)
> [30] And do not grieve the Holy Spirit of God, by whom you were sealed for the day of redemption.

7. A gift – the Holy Spirit cannot be bought, He is a gift

given by God to His children:

> Acts 2:38 (NKJV)
> [38] Then Peter said to them, "Repent, and let every one of you be baptized in the name of Jesus Christ for the remission of sins; and you shall receive the gift of the Holy Spirit.

4

Human Beings

In this chapter, we will look at some basic biblical truths about human beings.

Humans are made in the image of God:

> Genesis 1:26 (ESV)
> **26** Then God said, "Let us make man in our image, after our likeness. And let them have dominion over the fish of the sea and over the birds of the heavens and over the livestock and over all the earth and over every creeping thing that creeps on the earth."

> Genesis 1:27 (ESV)
> **27** So God created man in his own image,
> in the image of God he created him;
> male and female he created them.

The first man was called Adam. God made a wife for Adam, whom he later named Eve. She was to be his companion and helper:

> Genesis 2:18 (ESV)
> **18** Then the LORD God said, "It is not good that the man should be alone; I will make him a helper fit for him."

> Genesis 2:21-24 (ESV)
> **21** So the LORD God caused a deep sleep to fall upon the man, and while he slept took one of his ribs and closed up its place with flesh. **22** And the rib that the LORD God had taken from the man he made into a woman and brought her to the man. **23** Then the man said,
> "This at last is bone of my bones
> and flesh of my flesh;
> she shall be called Woman,
> because she was taken out of Man."
> **24** Therefore a man shall leave his father and his mother and hold fast to his wife, and they shall become one flesh.

Adam and Eve are the first example of a marriage. Whilst society has defined marriage in various ways over the years (including polygamous marriage), the first marriage in the Bible (Adam and Eve) was between one man and one woman. When Jesus commented on marriage, He cited "the beginning" as the standard we are to follow. For this reason, followers of Jesus accept marriage as the union between one man and one woman:

> Matthew 19:4-6 (ESV)
> **4** [Jesus] answered, "Have you not read that he who created them from the beginning made them male

and female, ⁵ and said, 'Therefore a man shall leave his father and his mother and hold fast to his wife, and the two shall become one flesh'? ⁶ So they are no longer two but one flesh. What therefore God has joined together, let not man separate."

When God created Adam, He placed him in the garden of Eden to look after it and permitted him to eat of any tree, except the tree of the knowledge of good and evil:

> Genesis 2:15-17 (ESV)
> ¹⁵ The LORD God took the man and put him in the garden of Eden to work it and keep it. ¹⁶ And the LORD God commanded the man, saying, "You may surely eat of every tree of the garden, ¹⁷ but of the tree of the knowledge of good and evil you shall not eat, for in the day that you eat of it you shall surely die."

The reason he was not to eat of the forbidden tree is because God wanted a relationship with him. Eating of the forbidden tree would mean that Adam would now be his own source of the knowledge of good and evil, instead of depending on God for the wisdom he needed. Indeed, every tree in the garden was described as "good for food" and "pleasant to the sight" (Genesis 2:9) but the marked difference about the forbidden tree was that it was also able to "make one wise" (Genesis 3:6) i.e. it was able to give wisdom, independent of a relationship with God.

The devil came to Adam's wife in the form of a serpent, and deceived her into eating from the forbidden tree. She then gave some of the fruit to Adam, and he ate it also:

Genesis 3:6 (ESV)
⁶So when the woman saw that the tree was good for food, and that it was a delight to the eyes, and that the tree was to be desired to make one wise, she took of its fruit and ate, and she also gave some to her husband who was with her, and he ate.

Although Adam and Eve did not die physically there and then, they instantly died spiritually when they partook of the fruit. Consequently, all their descendants are born spiritually dead (Ephesians 2:1). It was through this transgression that the devil gained his position of influence in the world. Since the disobedience of Adam and Eve, all human beings have been born with a sinful nature (i.e. an inclination towards sin). By "sin", we mean doing things that are wrong in God's sight:

Romans 7:14 (ESV)
¹⁴For we know that the law is spiritual, but I am of the flesh, sold under sin.

Romans 7:18 (ESV)
¹⁸For I know that nothing good dwells in me, that is, in my flesh. For I have the desire to do what is right, but not the ability to carry it out.

Romans 3:23 (ESV)
²³for all have sinned and fall short of the glory of God,

1 John 5:17 (ESV)
¹⁷All wrongdoing is sin...

Humans are comprised of spirit, soul and body:

> 1 Thessalonians 5:23 (ESV)
> [23] Now may the God of peace himself sanctify you completely, and may your whole spirit and soul and body be kept blameless at the coming of our Lord Jesus Christ.

The human spirit is the part of us that connects with God:

> John 4:24 (ESV)
> [24] God is spirit, and those who worship him must worship in spirit and truth."

The English word "psyche" is derived from the Greek word for "soul". The soul is the mind, will and emotions. Sometimes, the word "soul" is also used in the Bible simply refer to a person.

The body is the physical part of our being, and is where the sinful nature inherited from Adam resides:

> Romans 7:23 (HCSB)
> [23] But I see a different law in the parts of my body, waging war against the law of my mind and taking me prisoner to the law of sin in the parts of my body.

Because God loves us, He doesn't want to leave us in our fallen condition, and has therefore made salvation available to everyone, which we will look at in the next chapter:

> John 3:16 (ESV)
> [16] "For God so loved the world, that he gave his on-

ly Son, that whoever believes in him should not perish but have eternal life.

5

Salvation

In this chapter, we will look briefly at what salvation is.

Salvation is being rescued from the power and effects of sin.

> Matthew 1:21 (NKJV)
> [21] And she will bring forth a Son, and you shall call His name JESUS, for He will save His people from their sins."

Salvation is necessary because all humans have sinned.

> Romans 3:23 (NKJV)
> [23] for all have sinned and fall short of the glory of God,

Sin has affected our condition and our destination. Our condition is that we are slaves to sin, our destination is eternal damnation:

John 8:34 (NKJV)
[34] Jesus answered them, "Most assuredly, I say to you, whoever commits sin is a slave of sin.

Revelation 21:8 (NKJV)
[8] But the cowardly, unbelieving, abominable, murderers, sexually immoral, sorcerers, idolaters, and all liars shall have their part in the lake which burns with fire and brimstone, which is the second death."

Salvation rescues us from our fallen condition, and gives us the hope of eternal life with God instead of eternal damnation.

John 8:34–36 (NKJV)
[34] Jesus answered them, "Most assuredly, I say to you, whoever commits sin is a slave of sin. [35] And a slave does not abide in the house forever, *but* a son abides forever. [36] Therefore if the Son makes you free, you shall be free indeed.

John 3:16 (NKJV)
[16] For God so loved the world that He gave His only begotten Son, that whoever believes in Him should not perish but have everlasting life.

Salvation was achieved by the death and resurrection of Jesus Christ. In His death Jesus received the punishment we deserved so that we could go free. Because God is a God of justice, sin must be punished. Jesus received our punishment by dying for us on the cross. Through His resurrection we are given a new start:

Romans 5:8 (NKJV)
[8] But God demonstrates His own love toward us, in that while we were still sinners, Christ died for us.

1 Corinthians 15:3 (NKJV)
[3] For I delivered to you first of all that which I also received: that Christ died for our sins according to the Scriptures,

1 Peter 1:3 (NKJV)
[3] Blessed *be* the God and Father of our Lord Jesus Christ, who according to His abundant mercy has begotten us again to a living hope through the resurrection of Jesus Christ from the dead,

Salvation is received by repenting of our sins, and putting our faith in Jesus. Repentance means making a decision to turn away from sin:

Mark 1:15 (NKJV)
[15] and saying, "The time is fulfilled, and the kingdom of God is at hand. Repent, and believe in the gospel."

Acts 16:31 (NKJV)
[31] So they said, "Believe on the Lord Jesus Christ, and you will be saved, you and your household."

Ephesians 2:8 (NKJV)
[8] For by grace you have been saved through faith, and that not of yourselves; *it is* the gift of God,

Salvation is instantaneous - the moment we place our faith in Jesus Christ, we are forgiven of our sins, justified by God ("justified" means "declared righteous"), and given a new spiritual life:

> Ephesians 1:7 (NKJV)
> [7] In Him we have redemption through His blood, the forgiveness of sins, according to the riches of His grace

> Romans 5:1 (NKJV)
> Therefore, having been justified [i.e. declared righteous] by faith, we have peace with God through our Lord Jesus Christ,

> 1 John 5:12 (NKJV)
> [12] He who has the Son has life; he who does not have the Son of God does not have life.

Salvation is also progressive - our soul (i.e. mind, will and emotions) is progressively being transformed by the word of God:

> James 1:21 (NKJV)
> [21] Therefore lay aside all filthiness and overflow of wickedness, and receive with meekness the implanted word, which is able to save your souls.

> Romans 12:2 (NKJV)
> [2] And do not be conformed to this world, but be transformed by the renewing of your mind, that you may prove what *is* that good and acceptable and perfect will of God.

Salvation is also future - our bodies will be saved and made brand new when Jesus returns:

Philippians 3:20-21 (NKJV)
[20] For our citizenship is in heaven, from which we also eagerly wait for the Savior, the Lord Jesus Christ, [21] who will transform our lowly body that it may be conformed to His glorious body, according to the working by which He is able even to subdue all things to Himself.

Salvation can be lost if we do not continue in the faith

Romans 11:22 (NKJV)
[22] Therefore consider the goodness and severity of God: on those who fell, severity; but toward you, goodness, if you continue in *His* goodness. Otherwise you also will be cut off.

Matthew 24:13 (NKJV)
[13] But he who endures to the end shall be saved.

Salvation includes the fact that through Christ, we have become part of God's family, and can call God "Father" just like Jesus does. God is therefore called "the Father" by Christians.

Galatians 4:6 (NKJV)
[6] And because you are sons, God has sent forth the Spirit of His Son into your hearts, crying out, "Abba, Father!"

John 1:12-13 (NKJV)
[12] But as many as received Him, to them He gave the right to become children of God, to those who believe in His name: [13] who were born, not of blood,

nor of the will of the flesh, nor of the will of man, but of God.

Salvation also includes the fact that we are now delivered from the power of darkness, and are part of the kingdom of Christ:

> Colossians 1:13 (NKJV)
> [13] He has delivered us from the power of darkness and conveyed *us* into the kingdom of the Son of His love

Salvation also includes the fact that we are now spiritually united with Christ, and are spiritually seated with Him in the heavenly places:

> Ephesians 2:6 (NKJV)
> [6] and [God] raised *us* up together, and made *us* sit together in the heavenly *places* in Christ Jesus,

6

Grace vs. Law

In this chapter, we will continue our study of salvation by looking at grace vs. law.

To live successfully as a Christian, it is essential to realise that we are no longer under the Law of Moses. The Law of Moses is the 613 commandments that God gave to Israel under the leadership of Moses, after they came out of Egypt. This law is found from Exodus 20 through till the end of Deuteronomy. The law includes (but is not limited to) the Ten Commandments and covers moral conduct, religious festivals (feast days), Sabbaths, the protocols of sacrifices for atonement of sins, dietary laws, inheritance laws, and other regulations including the type of clothes you could wear and even how your beard must be kept. The Law of Moses will be referred to simply as "the law" in the rest of this chapter.

It is impossible to live under the law and under grace at the same time. Living under law, and living under grace are mutually exclusive options:

John 1:17 (NKJV)
[17] For the law was given through Moses, *but* grace and truth came through Jesus Christ.

Romans 6:14 (ESV)
[14] For sin will have no dominion over you, since you are not under law but under grace.

To be "under law" means that you have to obey the law in order to be righteous:

Romans 10:5 (ESV)
[5] For Moses writes about the righteousness that is based on the law, that the person who does the commandments shall live by them.

To be under grace means that righteousness is given to you as a free gift. Being declared righteous by God is called "justification":

Romans 3:24 (NKJV)
[24] being justified freely by His grace through the redemption that is in Christ Jesus,

The law is not the means of true righteousness. True righteousness is given to us by God when we put our faith in Jesus:

Galatians 2:16 (ESV)
[16] yet we know that a person is not justified by works of the law but through faith in Jesus Christ, so we also have believed in Christ Jesus, in order to be justified by faith in Christ and not by works

of the law, because by works of the law no one will be justified.

Believing in Christ puts an end to trying to be righteous by keeping the law:

> Romans 10:4 (ESV)
> [4] For Christ is the end of the law for righteousness to everyone who believes.

> Romans 3:28 (ESV)
> [28] For we hold that one is justified by faith apart from works of the law.

Now that Christ has come, our relationship with the law has changed. The following four observations describe how we should now view the law:

1. The law is a former guardian:

> Galatians 3:24-25 (ESV)
> [24] So then, the law was our guardian until Christ came, in order that we might be justified by faith. [25] But now that faith has come, we are no longer under a guardian,

The word "guardian" in the above passage has reference to a slave in a house, who was appointed to watch over the child on his way to school (to ensure that he got to school safely). The law was our guardian, to bring us safely to Christ so that we could be justified by faith. Now that we have been justified by faith, there is no more need for the guardian.

2. The law is obsolete (no longer in use):

> Hebrews 8:7–8, 13 (ESV)
> **⁷**For if that first covenant had been faultless, there would have been no occasion to look for a second.
> **⁸**For he finds fault with them when he says:
> "Behold, the days are coming, declares the Lord, when I will establish a new covenant...
> **¹³**In speaking of a new covenant, he makes the first one obsolete. And what is becoming obsolete and growing old is ready to vanish away.

3. The law is a previous spouse. In addition to ending a marriage, death also releases the surviving spouse to marry someone else. Paul uses this analogy with reference to our relationship with the law:

> Romans 7:4–6 (NKJV)
> **⁴**Therefore, my brethren, you also have become dead to the law through the body of Christ, that you may be married to another—to Him who was raised from the dead, that we should bear fruit to God.... **⁶**... we have been delivered from the law, having died to what we were held by, so that we should serve in the newness of the Spirit and not *in* the oldness of the letter.

Through the death of Jesus Christ, we have died to the law. This means that the law no longer has authority over us. Notice that we were only delivered from the law when Jesus died, and not before then. Therefore, before His death, Jesus made sure that His followers observed the law:

Matthew 5:17-18 (NKJV)
[17] "Do not think that I came to destroy the Law or the Prophets. I did not come to destroy but to fulfill. [18] For assuredly, I say to you, till heaven and earth pass away, one jot or one tittle will by no means pass from the law till all is fulfilled.

In other words, whilst the law was in force, His disciples were to keep it. But when Jesus died and rose again (thereby fulfilling the law) our relationship with the law ended. We have been united with Christ's death, so that we have died to the law. Our marriage has been ended through death, so that we could now have a new marriage with Christ.

In this new marriage, Paul says, we "serve in the newness of the Spirit and not *in* the oldness of the letter." We will look at that shortly.

4. We must not try to be justified by the law. Paul taught that if we try to be made righteous by keeping the law, we have fallen from grace:

Galatians 5:4 (NASB)
You have been severed from Christ, you who are seeking to be justified by law; you have fallen from grace.

A common misunderstanding is that the Ten Commandments are not part of the Law of Moses. However, the Ten Commandments are simply the first ten of the 613 commandments that comprise the Law of Moses, and are therefore part of it. Paul taught that the law we have been released from includes the Ten Commandments.

This is evident from the fact that the tenth command-ment ("you shall not covet") is stated as part of the law that Christ has released us from in the following passage:

> Romans 7:6-7 (ESV)
> [6]But now we are released from the law... I would not have known what it is to covet if the law had not said, "You shall not covet."

As Christians have been released from the whole law, it is wrong to insist that believers observe the Sabbath, Old Testament feast days and dietary laws:

> Colossians 2:16-17 (ESV)
> [16]Therefore let no one pass judgment on you in questions of food and drink, or with regard to a festival or a new moon or a Sabbath. [17]These are a shadow of the things to come, but the substance belongs to Christ.

Now that we have been released from the law, how are we to live righteously? We live righteously, not by following the written code of the law, but by following the Holy Spirit and walking in love. When we are led by the Holy Spirit, instead of by our flesh, we will live righteously:

> Romans 8:4 (ESV)
> [4]in order that the righteous requirement of the law might be fulfilled in us, who walk not according to the flesh but according to the Spirit.

> Galatians 5:22-23 (ESV)
> [22]But the fruit of the Spirit is love, joy, peace, pa-tience, kindness, goodness, faithfulness,

²³gentleness, self-control; against such things there is no law.

Galatians 5:14 (ESV)
¹⁴For the whole law is fulfilled in one word: "You shall love your neighbor as yourself."

Why are we made righteous through faith in Jesus Christ? The reason is because on the cross, Jesus became what we are so that through His resurrection we could become what He is. Our sin was transferred to Jesus on the cross and He paid the penalty for it there; but when He arose from the grave, He arose without any trace of sin: completely righteous. When we put our faith in Jesus, we are united with Him and therefore share in His righteousness which we receive as a free gift:

2 Corinthians 5:21 (ESV)
²¹For our sake he made him [Jesus] to be sin who knew no sin, so that in him we might become the righteousness of God.

Romans 4:25 (ESV)
²⁵[Jesus] was delivered up for our trespasses and raised for our justification.

Conclusion: under grace, we are given righteousness as a free gift through faith in Jesus Christ; and we live out that righteousness by walking in the Holy Spirit. We are no longer under the law.

7

The Church

In this chapter we will explore what the Bible has to say about the church.

The word "church" is a reference to all those who belong to Jesus Christ. In the Greek language, it was used with reference to an assembly of people. The word "church" is never used to refer to a building; it is always used with reference to people.

The church is referred to as the body of Christ. This metaphor emphasises the church's unity with Jesus Christ, who is the Head of the church. It also emphasises that every member of the church has an important function and is therefore to make a meaningful contribution using their various gifts (just like the various parts of our body):

Colossians 1:18 (NKJV)
[18] And He is the head of the body, the church, who is the beginning, the firstborn from the dead, that

in all things He may have the preeminence.

Romans 12:4-8 (NKJV)
[4] For as we have many members in one body, but all the members do not have the same function, [5] so we, *being* many, are one body in Christ, and individually members of one another. [6] Having then gifts differing according to the grace that is given to us, *let us use them:* if prophecy, *let us prophesy* in proportion to our faith; [7] or ministry, *let us use it* in *our* ministering; he who teaches, in teaching; [8] he who exhorts, in exhortation; he who gives, with liberality; he who leads, with diligence; he who shows mercy, with cheerfulness.

The church is also described as betrothed to Christ. First-century Jewish marriages began with a betrothal period that was legally binding. During this time, the couple was considered married and referred to as husband and wife even though they did not yet live together. This image emphasises that the church is looking forward to the coming of her bridegroom (Jesus Christ) and also indicates the necessity of the church to keep herself holy:

2 Corinthians 11:2 (NKJV)
[2] For I am jealous for you with godly jealousy. For I have betrothed you to one husband, that I may present *you as* a chaste virgin to Christ.

Ephesians 5:25 (NKJV)
[25] Husbands, love your wives, just as Christ also loved the church and gave Himself for her,

Ephesians 5:31–32 (NKJV)
[31] *"For this reason a man shall leave his father and mother and be joined to his wife, and the* two shall become one flesh." [32] This is a great mystery, but I speak concerning Christ and the church.

John 14:1–3 (ESV)
"Let not your hearts be troubled. Believe in God; believe also in me. [2] In my Father's house are many rooms. If it were not so, would I have told you that I go to prepare a place for you? [3] And if I go and prepare a place for you, I will come again and will take you to myself, that where I am you may be also.

The church is the army of God. For this reason, when Paul described our conflict, he did so by alluding to the armour worn by a Roman soldier. However, the church is not fighting against human beings, but against spiritual forces:

Ephesians 6:11–18 (NKJV)
[11] Put on the whole armor of God, that you may be able to stand against the wiles of the devil. [12] For we do not wrestle against flesh and blood, but against principalities, against powers, against the rulers of the darkness of this age, against spiritual *hosts* of wickedness in the heavenly *places.* [13] Therefore take up the whole armor of God, that you may be able to withstand in the evil day, and having done all, to stand. [14] Stand therefore, having girded your waist with truth, having put on the breastplate of righteousness, [15] and having shod your feet with the prepa-

ration of the gospel of peace; [16] above all, taking the shield of faith with which you will be able to quench all the fiery darts of the wicked one. [17] And take the helmet of salvation, and the sword of the Spirit, which is the word of God; [18] praying always with all prayer and supplication in the Spirit, being watchful to this end with all perseverance and supplication for all the saints—

The church is God's temple. This image points to the fact that God lives in the church. Not only are we God's temple, we are also the priests that serve in the temple:

> 2 Corinthians 6:16 (NKJV)
> [16] For you are the temple of the living God. As God has said:
> *"I will dwell in them*
> *And walk among them.*
> *I will be their God,*
> *And they shall be My people."*

> 1 Peter 2:5 (NKJV)
> [5] you also, as living stones, are being built up a spiritual house, a holy priesthood, to offer up spiritual sacrifices acceptable to God through Jesus Christ.

The basis for what the church does and believes is the teachings of Jesus Christ and the teachings of the founding apostles and prophets of the Christian faith. These teachings are found in the New Testament, and that is the foundation upon which we are to build:

Ephesians 2:20 (NKJV)
[20] having been built on the foundation of the apostles and prophets, Jesus Christ Himself being the chief corner*stone,*

The church is God's family. We are God's children, and He is our Father. Jesus, the eternal Son of God, is our Big Brother:

Ephesians 2:19 (NLT)
[19] So now you Gentiles are no longer strangers and foreigners. You are citizens along with all of God's holy people. You are members of God's family.

Romans 8:29 (NKJV)
[29] For whom He foreknew, He also predestined *to be* conformed to the image of His Son, that He might be the firstborn among many brethren.

The church is to preach the gospel to the entire world:

Mark 16:15 (NKJV)
[15] And He said to them, "Go into all the world and preach the gospel to every creature.

Jesus has commanded the church to baptise in water those who respond to the message of salvation. To "baptise" means to make fully wet. When an individual is baptised in water, it represents their burial with Jesus and the start of a new spiritual life. Water baptism is part of the required response to the gospel:

Matthew 28:18-20 (NKJV)
[18] And Jesus came and spoke to them, saying, "All

authority has been given to Me in heaven and on earth. [19] Go therefore and make disciples of all the nations, baptizing them in the name of the Father and of the Son and of the Holy Spirit, [20] teaching them to observe all things that I have commanded you; and lo, I am with you always, *even* to the end of the age." Amen.

Mark 16:15–16 (NKJV)

[15] And He said to them, "Go into all the world and preach the gospel to every creature. [16] He who believes and is baptized will be saved; but he who does not believe will be condemned.

Acts 2:38 (NKJV)

[38] Then Peter said to them, "Repent, and let every one of you be baptized in the name of Jesus Christ for the remission of sins; and you shall receive the gift of the Holy Spirit.

Romans 6:3–4 (NKJV)

[3] Or do you not know that as many of us as were baptized into Christ Jesus were baptized into His death? [4] Therefore we were buried with Him through baptism into death, that just as Christ was raised from the dead by the glory of the Father, even so we also should walk in newness of life.

In Matthew 28:19, Jesus commanded His disciples to baptise in the name of the Trinity ("in the name of the Father and of the Son and of the Holy Spirit"). In the book of Acts, we read that people were baptised in the name of Jesus (Acts 8:16; 19:5). There is no contradiction here. To do something in someone's name simply means to do it in their authority or on their behalf. When people are described as being baptised in the name of Jesus, it is not a reference to the formula used but simply means that those baptising them were doing so in Jesus' authority - after all, it was Jesus who commanded His disciples to baptise people. However, the particular words that were actually used when baptising were, "in the name of the Father, and of the Son, and of the Holy Spirit" (that the Trinitarian formula was used in baptism is also testified to in an early Christian writing called the *Didache*, 7:1-3).

Jesus has also commanded the church to observe Holy Communion in remembrance of Him:

> 1 Corinthians 11:23-26 (NKJV)
> [23] For I received from the Lord that which I also delivered to you: that the Lord Jesus on the *same* night in which He was betrayed took bread; [24] and when He had given thanks, He broke *it* and said, "Take, eat; this is My body which is broken for you; do this in remembrance of Me." [25] In the same manner *He* also *took* the cup after supper, saying, "This cup is the new covenant in My blood. This do, as often as you drink *it,* in remembrance of Me."
> [26] For as often as you eat this bread and drink this cup, you proclaim the Lord's death till He comes.

Church meetings should include worship, the teaching of God's word, prayer, fellowship, and the exercise of spiritual gifts:

1 Corinthians 14:26 (NKJV)
²⁶ How is it then, brethren? Whenever you come together, each of you has a psalm, has a teaching,
has a tongue, has a revelation, has an interpretation. Let all things be done for edification.

Acts 2:42 (NKJV)
⁴² And they continued steadfastly in the apostles'
doctrine and fellowship, in the breaking of bread,
and in prayers.

We have seen that the word "church" is a reference to
God's people. There are three levels at which God's
people are referred to as the "church"...

First, the word "church" is used of all the believers in the
world. We call this the universal church:

Ephesians 1:22 (NKJV)
²² And He [God] put all *things* under His [Jesus']
feet, and gave Him *to be* head over all *things* to the
church,

Second, the word "church" is also used of all the believers
in a city or town. We call this the city-church:

Acts 11:22 (NKJV)
²² Then news of these things came to the ears of
the church in Jerusalem, and they sent out Barna-
bas to go as far as Antioch.

Third, the word "church" is also used of a congregation
that meets in a house. The first century city- was thus
subdivided into house-churches. Excavations from that

period indicate that the atrium of larger homes could hold up to 36 people and courtyards could accommodate up to 200 people. The house-church is equivalent to what we would typically call the local church today:

> Romans 16:5 (NKJV)
> ⁵ Likewise *greet* the church that is in their house. Greet my beloved Epaenetus, who is the firstfruits of Achaia to Christ.

> 1 Corinthians 16:19 (NKJV)
> ¹⁹ The churches of Asia greet you. Aquila and Priscilla greet you heartily in the Lord, with the church that is in their house.

> Colossians 4:15 (NKJV)
> ¹⁵ Greet the brethren who are in Laodicea, and Nymphas and the church that *is* in his house.

> Philemon 2 (NKJV)
> ² to the beloved Apphia, Archippus our fellow soldier, and to the church in your house:

Each house-church had a leader. All the house-church leaders in a city were collectively known as the "elders" of the church in that city. This is similar to the fact that in ancient Israel, the most basic level of eldership was comprised of the heads of each household (see Exodus 12:21 where "all the elders of Israel" is a reference to every head of a household). Even so, the city-church eldership was made up of the leaders of each house-church. Because each house-church in a city had one elder, the city-church could be said to have "elders". Therefore, it is the city-church, not the house-church, to which the plural term "elders" applies. The verses below pertain to the eldership of the city-churches:

> Titus 1:5 (NKJV)
> [5] For this reason I left you in Crete, that you should set in order the things that are lacking, and appoint elders in every city as I commanded you—

> Acts 14:21–23 (NKJV)
> [21] And when they had preached the gospel to that city and made many disciples, they returned to Lystra, Iconium, and Antioch, [22] strengthening the souls of the disciples, exhorting *them* to continue in the faith, and *saying,* "We must through many tribulations enter the kingdom of God." [23] So when they had appointed elders in every church, and prayed with fasting, they commended them to the Lord in whom they had believed.

The city-church was a single community. Those who were part of the house-church saw themselves as part of the wider city-church, and Paul would address the city-wide church as a single entity, even though it was comprised of many house-churches:

> 1 Corinthians 1:2 (NKJV)
> [2] To the church of God which is at Corinth, to those who are sanctified in Christ Jesus, called *to be* saints, with all who in every place call on the name of Jesus Christ our Lord, both theirs and ours:

The word "elder" denoted the spiritual maturity of the house-church leader. The elders were also known as "pastors" and "overseers". These terms denoted the function of the elder, namely the pastoral responsibility of feeding the church with God's word, caring for and leading them; and the responsibility to oversee the church. The word "overseer" is translated "bishop" in some translations. In the first century church, a bishop (overseer) was simply a house-church leader:

> Acts 20:17-18, 28 (NIV)
> [17] From Miletus, Paul sent to Ephesus for the elders of the church. [18] When they arrived, he said to them: "...[28] Keep watch over yourselves and all the flock of which the Holy Spirit has made you overseers. Be shepherds [i.e. pastors] of the church of God, which he bought with his own blood.

> Ephesians 4:11 (NKJV)
> [11] And He Himself gave some *to be...* pastors

> Titus 1:5-7 (ESV)
> [5] This is why I left you in Crete, so that you might put what remained into order, and appoint elders in every town as I directed you— [6] if anyone is above reproach, the husband of one wife, and his children are believers and not open to the charge of debauchery or insubordination. [7] For an overseer, as God's steward, must be above reproach. He must not be arrogant or quick-tempered or a drunkard or violent or greedy for gain,

The house-church pastor was assisted by "deacons" who served in practical ways. Notice that in the following passage, "overseer" is singular whilst "deacons" is plural, indicating that there was one pastor and several deacons in each house-church. Notice also that there are strict criteria for those who may be appointed to these positions:

> 1 Timothy 3:1–13 (ESV)
> The saying is trustworthy: If anyone aspires to the office of overseer, he desires a noble task. ²Therefore an overseer must be above reproach, the husband of one wife, sober-minded, self-controlled, respectable, hospitable, able to teach, ³not a drunkard, not violent but gentle, not quarrelsome, not a lover of money. ⁴He must manage his own household well, with all dignity keeping his children submissive, ⁵for if someone does not know how to manage his own household, how will he care for God's church? ⁶He must not be a recent convert, or he may become puffed up with conceit and fall into the condemnation of the devil. ⁷Moreover, he must be well thought of by outsiders, so that he may not fall into disgrace, into a snare of the devil.
> ⁸Deacons likewise must be dignified, not double-tongued, not addicted to much wine, not greedy for dishonest gain. ⁹They must hold the mystery of the faith with a clear conscience. ¹⁰And let them also be tested first; then let them serve as deacons if they prove themselves blameless. ¹¹Their wives likewise must be dignified, not slanderers, but sober-minded, faithful in all things. ¹²Let deacons each be the husband of one wife, managing their children and their own households well. ¹³For those who serve well as deacons gain a good standing for themselves and also great confidence in the faith that is in Christ Jesus.

In the early church, the apostles provided leadership to the elders. However, the apostle Paul did not envision that the Ephesian elders would remain dependent upon him, but trained them so that they could function without him. Nonetheless, for reasons that aren't clear it seems that Paul found his way back to Ephesus and had to leave Timothy there to sort out problems that had arisen:

> Acts 20:25-27, 32 (NKJV)
> [25] "And indeed, now I know that you all, among whom I have gone preaching the kingdom of God, will see my face no more. [26] Therefore I testify to you this day that I *am* innocent of the blood of all *men*. [27] For I have not shunned to declare to you the whole counsel of God.... [32] "So now, brethren, I commend you to God and to the word of His grace, which is able to build you up and give you an inheritance among all those who are sanctified.

> 1 Timothy 1:3 (ESV)
> [3] As I urged you when I was going to Macedonia, remain at Ephesus so that you may charge certain persons not to teach any different doctrine,

Apart from apostles and pastors, there are other gifted people who provide leadership to the church:

> Ephesians 4:11 (NKJV)
> [11] And He Himself gave some *to be* apostles, some prophets, some evangelists, and some pastors and teachers,

Apostles laid the historic foundation for the church,

planted churches, served as missionaries and provided leadership to the church at large. Apostolic ministry today continues to do the last three of those functions but not the first as that was the domain of the founding apostles. Prophets communicate what God is presently saying to the church. Evangelists spread the gospel (and equip others to do the same), and teachers instruct people in the word of God. Some view the pastor and teacher as one and the same office (i.e. "pastor-teacher") whilst others view them as two distinct ministries. This author takes the view that they are two offices – there are some who are gifted to teach, but not gifted to pastor. As such, there are those who may have an itinerant teaching ministry without having the responsibility of overseeing a church.

Both men and women can occupy any leadership position in the church. Whilst senior leadership in the early church was predominately male, this must be understood in light of the fact that the first century world was patriarchal and should not be understood as prescriptive for all ages. The following passage has been misunderstood and therefore misused to restrict women from holding positions of authority in the church:

> 1 Timothy 2:12-14 (KJV)
> [12] But I suffer not a woman to teach, nor to usurp authority over the man, but to be in silence. [13] For Adam was first formed, then Eve. [14] And Adam was not deceived, but the woman being deceived was in the transgression.

When Paul wrote this, he was not banning women from teaching, but was prohibiting them from teaching in a manner that usurps authority over the men. False teachers who later became known as "the Gnostics" wrongly taught that Eve was created before Adam, was the source of knowledge, and was sent to be Adam's instructor (see the Gnostic document entitled *On the Origins of the World*). It would appear that an early form of this false teaching was circulating in Ephesus (where the letter containing this passage was sent). The women at Ephesus therefore thought they had a right to teach the men in a domineering manner. It is this type of domineering teaching that Paul is forbidding, which is affirmed by the phrase "nor to usurp authority over the man", which clarifies the type of teaching he is referring to. Paul is not forbidding normal teaching, but specifically teaching the men in an inappropriately domineering fashion. He corrects this by explaining that it was Adam that was created first, not Eve.

That God doesn't have a problem with women leaders is evident from the fact that Deborah, a prophetess, provided leadership to Israel (Judges 4:4-5). She even gave direction to the man Barak, the commander of Israel's army (Judges 4:6-7, 14). Also, Huldah, a prophetess, prophesied to men (2 Kings 22:14-20) and also gave them instruction (2 Kings 22:15, 18). There is also Priscilla (also known as Prisca), who with her husband Aquilla, explained the word of God to the man Apollos:

> Acts 18:26 (NKJV)
> [26] So he began to speak boldly in the synagogue. When Aquila and Priscilla [a woman] heard him, they took him aside and explained to him the way of God more accurately.

Paul certainly didn't have a problem with Priscilla, indeed he mentions her several times in his letters (Romans 16:3, 1 Corinthians 16:19, 2 Timothy 4:19). She is even called one of his co-workers:

> Romans 16:3 (ESV)
> ³Greet Prisca and Aquila, my fellow workers in Christ Jesus,

The fact that Priscilla was one of Paul's fellow workers meant that she would have had a position of authority in the church, to which others would have had to submit:

> 1 Corinthians 16:16 (NKJV)
> ¹⁶that you also submit to such, and to everyone who works and labors with *us.*

In the body of Christ, God anoints both men and women for His purposes:

> Acts 2:17-18 (NKJV)
> ¹⁷ *'And it shall come to pass in the last days, says God,*
> *That I will pour out of My Spirit on all flesh;*
> Your sons and your daughters shall prophesy,
> Your young men shall see visions,
> Your old men shall dream dreams.
> ¹⁸ *And on My menservants and on My maidservants*
> I will pour out My Spirit in those days;
> *And they shall prophesy.*

> Galatians 3:28 (NKJV)
> ²⁸There is neither Jew nor Greek, there is neither slave nor free, there is neither male nor female; for

you are all one in Christ Jesus.

8

The Baptism in the Holy Spirit

In this chapter, we will look at the baptism in the Holy Spirit.

There is a difference between having the Holy Spirit *within* you, and having the Holy Spirit *upon* you.

All Christians have the Holy Spirit *within* them. This happens automatically at salvation:

> Romans 8:9 (ESV)
> ⁹You, however, are not in the flesh but in the Spirit, if in fact the Spirit of God **dwells in you**. Anyone who does not have the Spirit of Christ does not belong to him.

Whilst all Christians have the Holy Spirit *within* them, not all Christians have the Holy Spirit *upon* them:

> Acts 8:14-16 (NKJV)
> ¹⁴Now when the apostles who were at Jerusalem

heard that Samaria had received the word of God, they sent Peter and John to them, [15] who, when they had come down, prayed for them that they might receive the Holy Spirit. [16] For as yet He had fallen **upon** none of them. They had only been baptized in the name of the Lord Jesus.

The Holy Spirit dwells *within* you for your salvation i.e. to seal you and make you a child of God:

Romans 8:15 (ESV)
[15] For you did not receive the spirit of slavery to fall back into fear, but you have received the Spirit of adoption as sons, by whom we cry, "Abba! Father!"

Galatians 4:6 (NKJV)
[6] And because you are sons, God has sent forth the Spirit of His Son into your hearts, crying out, "Abba, Father!"

Ephesians 1:13 (ESV)
[13] In him you also, when you heard the word of truth, the gospel of your salvation, and believed in him, were sealed with the promised Holy Spirit,

The Holy Spirit comes *upon* you to empower you for service. This is called being baptised in the Holy Spirit:

Acts 1:4–8 (ESV)
[4] And while staying with them he [Jesus] ordered them not to depart from Jerusalem, but to wait for the promise of the Father, which, he said, "you heard from me; [5] for John baptized with water, but

you will be baptized with the Holy Spirit not many days from now." **⁶**So when they had come together, they asked him, "Lord, will you at this time restore the kingdom to Israel?" **⁷**He said to them, "It is not for you to know times or seasons that the Father has fixed by his own authority. **⁸**But you will receive **power** when the Holy Spirit has come **upon** you, and you will be my witnesses in Jerusalem and in all Judea and Samaria, and to the end of the earth."

When the Holy Spirit comes within you automatically at salvation it is a quiet experience. However, when the Holy Spirit comes upon you, it is a loud experience accompanied by speaking in tongues. The word "tongues" simply means languages. When you are baptised in the Holy Spirit, the Holy Spirit enables you to speak in languages you have never learned. These languages can be either human or angelic (1 Corinthians 13:1):

Acts 2:1–4 (NKJV)
When the Day of Pentecost had fully come, they were all with one accord in one place. ²And suddenly there came a sound from heaven, as of a rushing mighty wind, and it filled the whole house where they were sitting. ³Then there appeared to them divided tongues, as of fire, and *one* sat upon each of them. ⁴And they were all filled with the Holy Spirit and began to speak with other tongues, as the Spirit gave them utterance.

Acts 10:44–46 (NKJV)
⁴⁴While Peter was still speaking these words, the Holy Spirit fell upon all those who heard the word.

⁴⁵ And those of the circumcision [the Jews] who believed were astonished, as many as came with Peter, because the gift of the Holy Spirit had been poured out on the Gentiles also. ⁴⁶ For they heard them speak with tongues and magnify God.

Acts 19:5-7 (NKJV)
⁵ When they heard *this,* they were baptized in the name of the Lord Jesus. ⁶ And when Paul had laid hands on them, the Holy Spirit came upon them, and they spoke with tongues and prophesied. ⁷ Now the men were about twelve in all.

In the book of Acts, each time Luke (the author) actually describes what happens when someone received the baptism in the Holy Spirit, speaking in tongues is always mentioned. If you have not yet received the baptism in the Holy Spirit with the evidence of speaking in tongues, you should ask God for it so that you can receive power to be a witness for Jesus:

Luke 11:13 (ESV)
¹³ If you then, who are evil, know how to give good gifts to your children, how much more will the heavenly Father give the Holy Spirit to those who ask him!"

There has been a lot of controversy in the church about speaking in tongues. This is mainly due to not understanding that there are three different functions of tongues.

First of all, tongues are the consistent sign that accompanies receiving the baptism in the Holy Spirit as we have seen above.

Secondly, tongues is a personal gift that Christians can use in prayer to strengthen themselves in the Lord:

> 1 Corinthians 14:14 (ESV)
> [14] For if I pray in a tongue, my spirit prays...

> 1 Corinthians 14:4 (ESV)
> [4] The one who speaks in a tongue builds up himself...

Thirdly, tongues is a ministry gift. This type of tongues is a public utterance in a church meeting that can then be supernaturally interpreted so that the church can benefit from it (1 Corinthians 14:27). Not everyone will have the ministry gift of tongues, and it is to this that Paul referred in the following passage where the context is clearly ministry:

> 1 Corinthians 12:29–30 (ESV)
> [29] Are all apostles? Are all prophets? Are all teachers? Do all work miracles? [30] Do all possess gifts of healing? Do all speak with tongues? Do all interpret?

However, tongues as an accompanying sign upon receiving the baptism in the Spirit, and as a personal gift that one can use in prayer is available to everyone:

> 1 Corinthians 14:5 (ESV)
> [5] Now I want you all to speak in tongues...

Here are four simple steps that you can take to receive the baptism with the Holy Spirit:

1. Get into the presence of Jesus Christ through praise and worship

When you were baptized in water, you had to get into the pool so that the baptizer could baptize you. If you want to be baptized in the Holy Spirit, then you need to get into the presence of Jesus, as He is the one who baptizes in the Holy Spirit (Matthew 3:11). An excellent way of entering His presence is by praising Him:

> Psalm 100:4 (NKJV)
> Enter into His gates with thanksgiving,
> And into His courts with praise.
> Be thankful to Him, and bless His name.

2. Ask God to fill you with His Spirit

Once you are in the presence of Jesus, ask God to fill you with the Holy Spirit. Jesus said:

> Luke 11:13 (NKJV)
> If you then, being evil, know how to give good gifts to your children, how much more will your heavenly Father give the Holy Spirit to those who ask Him!

3. Believe that you have received the baptism in the Holy Spirit

Once you have asked God to fill you with His Spirit, believe that God has done it. Jesus said:

Mark 11:24 (NKJV)
Whatever things you ask when you pray, believe that you receive them, and you will have them.

This is very important. Once you have asked God to fill you with His Spirit, you must believe that He has done so; you must accept and believe that it is done. Verbalize your faith by saying, "I believe I have received, thank You Lord for filling me with Your Spirit". Then you can move on to the next step.

4. Stop speaking in your own language, and by faith, begin to speak in other tongues

The Holy Spirit will not force you to speak in tongues. Notice that in Acts 2:4, the Bible doesn't say that the Holy Spirit spoke in tongues, it says that "they" (i.e. those who were filled) spoke in tongues:

Acts 2:4 (NKJV)
And they... began to speak with other tongues, as the Spirit gave them utterance.

When Jesus came walking on water to the disciples, He didn't force Peter to get out of the boat and start walking on the water:

Matthew 14:26-29 (NKJV)
And when the disciples saw Him walking on the sea, they were troubled, saying, "It is a ghost!" And they cried out for fear. But immediately Jesus spoke to them, saying, "Be of good cheer! It is I; do not be afraid." And Peter answered Him and said,

"Lord, if it is You, command me to come to You on the water." So He said, "Come." And when Peter had come down out of the boat, he walked on the water to go to Jesus.

Peter had to make a decision to get out of the boat, and then to walk on water. Peter had to leave what he knew (the boat) and step out into the unknown (the water). Peter didn't know He could walk on water until He tried, and you won't know you can speak in tongues until you try. So, you need to stop speaking in your own language (get out of the boat, leave the known) and start speaking the syllables that flow forth from your spirit (walk on water, you don't know you can until you put your foot on the water and try!). You won't necessarily hear new words in your mind. You just need to start speaking in faith the syllables that will flow forth from your spirit, and God will form them into your new prayer language. Just trust Him, He will do it!

If you have not yet received the baptism with the Holy Spirit, then I encourage you to take the time right now to follow those four steps, and to allow God to fill you with His Spirit.

9

Healing

In this chapter, we will look at what the Bible teaches about healing.

God is our Healer:

> Exodus 15:26 (ESV)
> ²⁶ saying, "If you will diligently listen to the voice of the LORD your God, and do that which is right in his eyes, and give ear to his commandments and keep all his statutes, I will put none of the diseases on you that I put on the Egyptians, for I am the LORD, your healer."

> Psalm 103:2-3 (ESV)
> ² Bless the LORD, O my soul,
> and forget not all his benefits,
> ³ who forgives all your iniquity,
> who heals all your diseases,

Jesus demonstrated God's heart towards the sick by

supernaturally healing everyone who came to Him for healing. Jesus shows us what God is like, and so we see through Jesus's ministry that it is always God's will to heal the sick:

> Matthew 4:23 (ESV)
> ²³ And he went throughout all Galilee, teaching in their synagogues and proclaiming the gospel of the kingdom and healing every disease and every affliction among the people.

> Mark 1:40-42 (ESV)
> ⁴⁰ And a leper came to him, imploring him, and kneeling said to him, "If you will, you can make me clean." ⁴¹ Moved with pity, he stretched out his hand and touched him and said to him, "I will; be clean." ⁴² And immediately the leprosy left him, and he was made clean.

> John 14:9 (ESV)
> ⁹ Jesus said to him, "Have I been with you so long, and you still do not know me, Philip? Whoever has seen me has seen the Father. How can you say, 'Show us the Father'?

Jesus has also given the ministry of supernatural healing to the church:

> John 14:12 (ESV)
> ¹² "Truly, truly, I say to you, whoever believes in me will also do the works that I do; and greater works than these will he do, because I am going to the Father.

Mark 16:15-18 (ESV)
¹⁵And he [Jesus] said to them, "Go into all the world and proclaim the gospel to the whole creation. ¹⁶Whoever believes and is baptized will be saved, but whoever does not believe will be condemned. ¹⁷And these signs will accompany those who believe.... ¹⁸ ...they will lay their hands on the sick, and they will recover."

Luke 10:9 (ESV)
⁹Heal the sick in it [the town] and say to them, 'The kingdom of God has come near to you.'

Jesus did not only suffer for our forgiveness, He also suffered so that we could be healed, making questioning whether or not it is God's will to heal someone as redundant as questioning whether or not it is God's will to save someone :

Isaiah 53:4-5 (NRSV)
⁴ Surely he [Jesus] has borne our infirmities
and carried our diseases;
yet we accounted him stricken,
struck down by God, and afflicted.
⁵ But he was wounded for our transgressions,
crushed for our iniquities;
upon him was the punishment that made us whole,
and by his bruises we are healed.

Matthew 8:17 (ESV)
¹⁷This was to fulfill what was spoken by the prophet Isaiah: "He took our illnesses and bore our diseases."

Passages in the New Testament that speak about Christian suffering are not about sickness; they are referring to persecution. We should not use such passages to explain sickness - suffering persecution and sickness are two different things.

> 2 Timothy 3:12 (NKJV)
> [12] Yes, and all who desire to live godly in Christ Jesus will suffer persecution.

Notice that suffering and sickness are dealt with separately in the following passage:

> James 5:13-15 (ESV)
> [13] Is anyone among you suffering? Let him pray...
> Is anyone cheerful? Let him sing praise. [14] Is anyone among you sick? Let him call for the elders of the church... [15] And the prayer of faith will save the one who is sick, and the Lord will raise him up...

Paul's "thorn in the flesh" was not a sickness. It was a reference to a demonic angel that was stirring up persecution against him. The phrase, "thorn in the flesh", was an idiom for something annoying, much like we use the phrase, "a pain in the neck".

> 2 Corinthians 12:7-10 (ESV)
> [7] So to keep me from becoming conceited because of the surpassing greatness of the revelations, a thorn was given me in the flesh, a messenger of Satan to harass me, to keep me from becoming conceited... [10] For the sake of Christ, then, I am

content with weaknesses, insults, hardships, persecutions, and calamities. For when I am weak, then I am strong.

Numbers 33:55 (ESV)
⁵⁵ But if you do not drive out the inhabitants of the land from before you, then those of them whom you let remain shall be as barbs in your eyes and thorns in your sides, and they shall trouble you in the land where you dwell.

However, Christians are not immune to sickness. Therefore, we should follow the natural laws of health if we will live healthy lives:

Philippians 2:27–30 (ESV)
²⁷ Indeed he was ill, near to death. But God had mercy on him, and not only on him but on me also, lest I should have sorrow upon sorrow. ²⁸ I am the more eager to send him, therefore, that you may rejoice at seeing him again, and that I may be less anxious. ²⁹ So receive him in the Lord with all joy, and honor such men, ³⁰ for he nearly died for the work of Christ, risking his life to complete what was lacking in your service to me.

1 Timothy 5:23 (ESV)
²³ (No longer drink only water, but use a little wine for the sake of your stomach and your frequent ailments.)

Sometimes, sickness may have a spiritual cause:

1 Corinthians 11:29-32 (ESV)

²⁹ For anyone who eats and drinks [Holy Communion] without discerning the body eats and drinks judgment on himself. ³⁰ That is why many of you are weak and ill, and some have died. ³¹ But if we judged ourselves truly, we would not be judged. ³² But when we are judged by the Lord, we are disciplined so that we may not be condemned along with the world.

James 5:15 (ESV)

¹⁵ And the prayer of faith will save the one who is sick, and the Lord will raise him up. And if he has committed sins, he will be forgiven.

We can receive supernatural healing by asking God to heal us, or by receiving prayer from Christians:

John 16:24 (ESV)

²⁴ Until now you have asked nothing in my name. Ask, and you will receive, that your joy may be full.

James 5:16 (ESV)

¹⁶ Therefore, confess your sins to one another and pray for one another, that you may be healed. The prayer of a righteous person has great power as it is working.

In severe cases, if the believer is bed bound, he or she is to call for church leaders to pray for him / her:

James 5:14-15 (ESV)

¹⁴ Is anyone among you sick? Let him call for the

elders of the church, and let them pray over him, anointing him with oil in the name of the Lord. **¹⁵** And the prayer of faith will save the one who is sick, and the Lord will raise him up. And if he has committed sins, he will be forgiven.

Sometimes, despite our prayers, a Christian may not be healed for reasons unknown to us. For example, it would seem that Paul was not able to heal Trophimus (2 Timothy 4:20). In cases where a Christian is not healed, and it is unclear why, we should not blame God or claim it wasn't God's will to heal that person. Instead we should simply say, "We don't know why", and continue to believe that God is good.

> Deuteronomy 29:29 (ESV)
> **²⁹** "The secret things belong to the LORD our God, but the things that are revealed belong to us and to our children forever, that we may do all the words of this law.

> 2 Timothy 4:20 (ESV)
> **²⁰** Erastus remained at Corinth, and I left Trophimus, who was ill, at Miletus.

We look forward to the return of Jesus Christ when we will receive new incorruptible bodies that will never get sick:

> 1 Corinthians 15:53 (NKJV)
> ⁵³ For this corruptible must put on incorruption, and this mortal *must* put on immortality.

Christians should not feel that they cannot go to doctors

for help. We thank God for both natural and supernatural healing:

> Colossians 4:14 (ESV)
> ¹⁴Luke the beloved physician greets you, as does Demas.

> 1 Timothy 5:23 (ESV)
> ²³(No longer drink only water, but use a little wine for the sake of your stomach and your frequent ailments.)

Here is an approach you can use when praying for the sick:

1. Ask the person what they believe will happen when I pray for them. Jesus said, "If you can believe, all things are possible to him who believes" (Mark 9:23 NKJV)

2. If appropriate, lay hands on the affected area of the body. If not, then lay your hand on their shoulder if they are happy for you to do so. Jesus said we would "lay hands on the sick, and they will recover" (Mark 16:18 NKJV)

3. Ask the Holy Spirit to come on the affected area. It is His power that does the healing! (Acts 10:38)

4. Command the sickness / pain to leave by authoritatively saying, "Out, in Jesus' name", believing that they are being healed as you speak. Jesus told us that we can speak directly to the mountain and it would obey us if we speak with faith in our heart (Mark 11:23).

5. Ask the person to test the condition immediately (if it is something they can test there and then). Jesus encouraged people to participate in their healing (Luke 6:10). If the condition is completely better, praise God! If they say it is a bit better, command the remaining discomfort to leave (if they are comfortable for you to continue) and get them to test it again.

If someone is not healed, never blame them or make them feel bad. Honour the person's dignity at all times. They should go away feeling encouraged, not condemned.

10

Angels and Heavenly Beings

In this chapter, we will explore the nature and work of angels.

Angels are spiritual beings created by Jesus Christ:

> Colossians 1:16 (ESV)
> 16 For by him [Jesus] all things were created, in heaven and on earth, visible and invisible, whether thrones or dominions or rulers or authorities—all things were created through him and for him.

> Hebrews 1:14 (ESV)
> 14 Are they [angels] not all ministering spirits...

Angels cannot die:

> Luke 20:36 (ESV)
> 36 [those who have been resurrected] cannot die anymore, because they are equal to angels and are sons of God, being sons of the resurrection.

Angels are numerous:

> Hebrews 12:22 (ESV)
> ²²But you have come to Mount Zion and to the city of the living God, the heavenly Jerusalem, and to innumerable angels in festal gathering,

Angels do not marry:

> Matthew 22:30 (ESV)
> ³⁰For in the resurrection they neither marry nor are given in marriage, but are like angels in heaven.

Angels are organised. For example, the angel Michael is called an "archangel" which means "chief angel", indicating that there is rank and order amongst the angels:

> Jude 9 (ESV)
> ⁹But when the archangel Michael...

Angels are obedient to God:

> Psalm 103:20 (ESV)
> ²⁰ Bless the LORD, O you his angels,
> you mighty ones who do his word,
> obeying the voice of his word!

The angels worship God and His Son Jesus Christ:

> Revelation 7:11 (ESV)
> ¹¹And all the angels were standing around the throne and around the elders and the four living

creatures, and they fell on their faces before the throne and worshiped God,

Hebrews 1:6 (ESV)
⁶And again, when he brings the firstborn [Jesus] into the world, he says,
"Let all God's angels worship him."

The angels are strong. They are called "mighty ones" (Psalm 103:20).

The angels are "holy" (i.e. "set apart"). The angels are set apart by and for God:

Luke 9:26 (ESV)
²⁶For whoever is ashamed of me and of my words, of him will the Son of Man be ashamed when he comes in his glory and the glory of the Father and of the holy angels.

The angels execute judgement on behalf of God:

2 Kings 19:35 (ESV)
³⁵And that night the angel of the LORD went out and struck down 185,000 in the camp of the Assyrians. And when people arose early in the morning, behold, these were all dead bodies.

The word "angel" means "messenger". God uses angels to give messages to people:

Acts 10:3-6 (ESV)
³About the ninth hour of the day he saw clearly in a vision an angel of God come in and say to him,

"Cornelius." ⁴And he stared at him in terror and said, "What is it, Lord?" And he said to him, "Your prayers and your alms have ascended as a memorial before God. ⁵And now send men to Joppa and bring one Simon who is called Peter. ⁶He is lodging with one Simon, a tanner, whose house is by the sea."

Angels are sent by God to be of service to His people:

> Hebrews 1:14 (ESV)
> ¹⁴Are they [angels] not all ministering spirits sent out to serve for the sake of those who are to inherit salvation?

> Psalm 34:7 (ESV)
> ⁷ The angel of the LORD encamps
> around those who fear him, and delivers them.

We are not to worship angels:

> Revelation 19:10 (ESV)
> ¹⁰Then I fell down at his [the angel's] feet to worship him, but he said to me, "You must not do that! I am a fellow servant with you and your brothers who hold to the testimony of Jesus. Worship God." For the testimony of Jesus is the spirit of prophecy.

In addition to angels, there are four other heavenly beings mentioned in the Bible...

1. Cherubim. "Cherubim" is the plural for "cherub". They are described as having four faces (on each side of their

head) so that they never need to turn around (their four faces mean that they can see in all directions). They have four wings and seem to be God's mode of transportation:

> Ezekiel 10:8 (ESV)
> [8] The cherubim appeared to have the form of a human hand under their wings.

> Ezekiel 10:14 (ESV)
> [14] And every one had four faces: the first face was the face of the cherub, and the second face was a human face, and the third the face of a lion, and the fourth the face of an eagle.

> Ezekiel 10:21 (ESV)
> [21] Each had four faces, and each four wings, and underneath their wings the likeness of human hands.

> Psalm 18:10 (ESV)
> [10] He rode on a cherub and flew;
> he came swiftly on the wings of the wind.

2. Seraphim. This word literally means "burning ones" which may describe their fiery appearance. They have six wings:

> Isaiah 6:1-3 (ESV)
> In the year that King Uzziah died I saw the Lord sitting upon a throne, high and lifted up; and the train of his robe filled the temple. [2] Above him stood the seraphim. Each had six wings: with two he covered his face, and with two he covered his feet, and with two he flew. [3] And one called to an-

other and said:
"Holy, holy, holy is the LORD of hosts;
the whole earth is full of his glory!"

3. The Four Living Creatures. These have six wings like the Seraphim, and each has the appearance of one of the four faces of the Cherubim. They are worshipping God continuously:

> Revelation 4:6–8 (ESV)
> [6] and before the throne there was as it were a sea of glass, like crystal.
> And around the throne, on each side of the throne, are four living creatures, full of eyes in front and behind: [7] the first living creature like a lion, the second living creature like an ox, the third living creature with the face of a man, and the fourth living creature like an eagle in flight. [8] And the four living creatures, each of them with six wings, are full of eyes all around and within, and day and night they never cease to say,
> "Holy, holy, holy, is the Lord God Almighty,
> who was and is and is to come!"

4. The 24 Elders. They seem to be senior persons who are seated before God's throne:

> Revelation 4:4 (ESV)
> [4] Around the throne were twenty-four thrones, and seated on the thrones were twenty-four elders, clothed in white garments, with golden crowns on their heads.

11

The Enemy

In this chapter, we will look at what the Bible says about our spiritual enemy.

The Bible reveals, that in the distant past, there were spiritual beings who rebelled against God. The leader of these rebels is referred to in various ways, including the following:

1. **Satan** (Mathew 4:10). This name means "adversary", and depicts him as the enemy of God and His people. In this capacity, he seeks to oppose the preaching of the gospel and inspires the persecution of God's people (1 Thessalonians 2:18; Revelation 2:10). He also hates humanity in general and dispatches wicked spirits to cause sickness and mental affliction (Luke 8:26-35; 13:11).
2. **The devil** (Matthew 4:1). This name means "slanderer" and points to the fact that he makes malicious statements about God and man. In fact, the devil is described as accusing us day and night before God (Revelation 12:10)

3. **That old serpent** (Revelation 12:9). This reveals the true identity of the serpent that deceived Eve in the garden of Eden.

4. **The tempter** (Matthew 4:3). This points to one of his chief activities – he tempts people to sin against God.

5. **The god of this world** (2 Corinthians 4:4). This designation reveals that currently, this world system is run by the devil. That is why as Christians we are told to "not be conformed to this world" (Romans 12:2). The devil's current position of influence was gained through the transgression of Adam in the garden of Eden.

6. **The deceiver of the whole world** (Revelation 12:9). This description of Satan reveals why the majority of people have not repented of their sins and turned to God – they are deceived by Satan.

Some of the angelic rebels found the women on earth beautiful to behold, and had intercourse with them, which resulted in the women giving birth to giants. These angels have been confined to a place called Tartarus until the day of judgement. Their offspring were killed in the flood that occurred in the time of Noah:

> Genesis 6:1–2 (NKJV)
> Now it came to pass, when men began to multiply on the face of the earth, and daughters were born to them, ²that the sons of God saw the daughters of men, that they *were* beautiful; and they took wives for themselves of all whom they chose.

> Genesis 6:4 (NKJV)
> ⁴There were giants on the earth in those days, and also afterward, when the sons of God came in to the daughters of men and they bore *children* to

them. Those *were* the mighty men who *were* of old, men of renown.

2 Peter 2:4 (HCSB)
⁴ For if God didn't spare the angels who sinned but threw them down into Tartarus and delivered them to be kept in chains of darkness until judgment;

However, not all of the angelic rebels were involved in that, and so there are still wicked spiritual beings at work in the world today.

The devil's cohorts seem to be an organised army and are referred to by various names according to their function: including principalities, powers, rulers of darkness, spiritual wickedness, demons, evil spirits, unclean spirits etc. (Ephesians 6:12, Luke 8:2;9:42;10:17)

However, when Jesus came, the devil and his cohorts had no authority over him. Instead, Jesus had total authority over them:

Matthew 8:16 (ESV)
¹⁶ That evening they brought to him many who were oppressed by demons, and he cast out the spirits with a word and healed all who were sick.

Mark 1:32-34 (ESV)
³² That evening at sundown they brought to him all who were sick or oppressed by demons. ³³ And the whole city was gathered together at the door. ³⁴ And he healed many who were sick with various diseases, and cast out many demons. And he

would not permit the demons to speak, because they knew him.

Through Christ, God has rescued believers from the devil's power:

> Colossians 1:13 (ESV)
> **13** He has delivered us from the domain of darkness and transferred us to the kingdom of his beloved Son,

Jesus has given those who believe in Him authority over Satan:

> Luke 10:19 (NKJV)
> 19 Behold, I give you the authority to trample on serpents and scorpions, and over all the power of the enemy, and nothing shall by any means hurt you.

We defeat the devil's accusations by the blood of Jesus, which was shed for the forgiveness of our sins. We rescue people from the devil's grip through preaching the gospel to them. We overcome his persecutions by being willing to die for Christ:

> Revelation 12:11 (NKJV)
> 11 And they overcame him by the blood of the Lamb and by the word of their testimony [i.e. preaching the gospel], and they did not love their lives to the death.

We are protected from the devil's attacks by wearing the whole armour of God:

Ephesians 6:10–18 (NKJV)
[10] Finally, my brethren, be strong in the Lord and in the power of His might. [11] Put on the whole armor of God, that you may be able to stand against the wiles of the devil. [12] For we do not wrestle against flesh and blood, but against principalities, against powers, against the rulers of the darkness of this age, against spiritual *hosts* of wickedness in the heavenly *places.* [13] Therefore take up the whole armor of God, that you may be able to withstand in the evil day, and having done all, to stand.
[14] Stand therefore, having girded your waist with truth, having put on the breastplate of righteousness, [15] and having shod your feet with the preparation of the gospel of peace; [16] above all, taking the shield of faith with which you will be able to quench all the fiery darts of the wicked one. [17] And take the helmet of salvation, and the sword of the Spirit, which is the word of God; [18] praying always with all prayer and supplication in the Spirit, being watchful to this end with all perseverance and supplication for all the saints—

We are protected from his deceptions by loving the truth of God's word:

2 Thessalonians 2:9–10 (NKJV)
[9] The coming of the *lawless one* is according to the working of Satan, with all power, signs, and lying wonders, [10] and with all unrighteous deception among those who perish, because they did not receive the love of the truth, that they might be saved.

We overcome his temptations by resisting him, praying, and walking in the Spirit

> James 4:7 (NKJV)
> [7] Therefore submit to God. Resist the devil and he will flee from you.

> Matthew 26:41 (NKJV)
> [41] Watch and pray, lest you enter into temptation. The spirit indeed *is* willing, but the flesh *is* weak."

> Galatians 5:16 (NKJV)
> [16] I say then: Walk in the Spirit, and you shall not fulfill the lust of the flesh.

The ultimate destiny of the devil and his angels is the everlasting fire that has been prepared for them:

> Matthew 25:41 (NKJV)
> [41] ...the everlasting fire prepared for the devil and his angels:

12

Prayer

In this chapter, we will look at some of the basic biblical truths about prayer.

Prayer is simply calling upon God:

> Genesis 26:25 (ESV)
> ²⁵ So he built an altar there and called upon the name of the LORD and pitched his tent there. And there Isaac's servants dug a well.

Prayer gives us the opportunity to praise and thank God:

> Philippians 4:6-7 (ESV)
> ⁶ do not be anxious about anything, but in everything by prayer and supplication with thanksgiving let your requests be made known to God. ⁷ And the peace of God, which surpasses all understanding, will guard your hearts and your minds in Christ Jesus.

Psalm 105:1 (ESV)
Oh give thanks to the LORD; call upon his name;

Prayer gives us the opportunity to draw near to God:

Psalm 145:18 (ESV)
18 The LORD is near to all who call on him,
to all who call on him in truth.

Prayer gives us the opportunity to makes requests and inquire of God:

John 16:24 (ESV)
24Until now you have asked nothing in my name. Ask, and you will receive, that your joy may be full.

Jeremiah 33:3 (ESV)
3Call to me and I will answer you, and will tell you great and hidden things that you have not known.

If we have committed a sin, prayer can also give us the opportunity to confess that sin to God and know that we are forgiven:

1 John 1:9 (ESV)
9If we confess our sins, he is faithful and just to forgive us our sins and to cleanse us from all un-righteousness.

When we pray, it is essential that we do so in faith. Faith means that we fully expect God to actually answer our prayer:

Matthew 21:22 (ESV)
²²And whatever you ask in prayer, you will receive, if you have faith."

Prayer must never just be done with our mouth. Our heart must also be fully engaged in our prayer – we must pray with the whole heart:

Psalm 119:145 (ESV)
¹⁴⁵ With my whole heart I cry; answer me, O LORD! I will keep your statutes.

All three persons in the Trinity are involved in prayer. We are to pray to God the Father, in the name of His Son, and in the power of the Holy Spirit:

John 16:23 (ESV)
²³In that day you will ask nothing of me [Jesus]. Truly, truly, I say to you, whatever you ask of the Father in my name, he will give it to you.

Jude 20 (ESV)
²⁰But you, beloved, building yourselves up in your most holy faith and praying in the Holy Spirit,

We should engage in individual, personal prayer:

Matthew 6:6 (ESV)
⁶But when you pray, go into your room and shut the door and pray to your Father who is in secret. And your Father who sees in secret will reward you.

We should also pray with other believers:

Acts 2:42 (NKJV)
⁴²And they continued steadfastly in the apostles'
doctrine and fellowship, in the breaking of bread,
and in prayers.

Here are seven hindrances to effective prayer:

1. Unbelief:

James 1:6-7 (ESV)
⁶But let him ask in faith, with no doubting, for the
one who doubts is like a wave of the sea that is
driven and tossed by the wind. ⁷For that person
must not suppose that he will receive anything
from the Lord;

2. Self-righteousness and pride:

Luke 18:9-14 (ESV)
⁹He also told this parable to some who trusted in
themselves that they were righteous, and treated
others with contempt: ¹⁰"Two men went up into
the temple to pray, one a Pharisee and the other a
tax collector. ¹¹The Pharisee, standing by himself,
prayed thus: 'God, I thank you that I am not like
other men, extortioners, unjust, adulterers, or
even like this tax collector. ¹²I fast twice a week; I
give tithes of all that I get.' ¹³But the tax collector,
standing far off, would not even lift up his eyes to
heaven, but beat his breast, saying, 'God, be merci-
ful to me, a sinner!' ¹⁴I tell you, this man went
down to his house justified, rather than the other.
For everyone who exalts himself will be humbled,

but the one who humbles himself will be exalted."

3. Wrong motives:

James 4:3 (ESV)
You ask and do not receive, because you ask wrongly, to spend it on your passions.

4. Not honouring your wife:

1 Peter 3:7 (ESV)
[7]Likewise, husbands, live with your wives in an understanding way, showing honor to the woman as the weaker vessel, since they are heirs with you of the grace of life, so that your prayers may not be hindered.

5. Unforgiveness and anger:

Matthew 6:14-15 (ESV)
[14]For if you forgive others their trespasses, your heavenly Father will also forgive you, [15]but if you do not forgive others their trespasses, neither will your Father forgive your trespasses.

1 Timothy 2:8 (ESV)
[8]I desire then that in every place the men should pray, lifting holy hands without anger or quarreling;

6. Not walking in love towards others:

1 John 3:22-23 (ESV)
[22]and whatever we ask we receive from him,

because we keep his commandments and do what pleases him. ²³ And this is his commandment, that we believe in the name of his Son Jesus Christ and love one another, just as he has commanded us.

7. Walking in unrighteousness:

James 5:16 (ESV)
¹⁶ Therefore, confess your sins to one another and pray for one another, that you may be healed. The prayer of a righteous person has great power as it is working.

13

Worship

In this chapter, we will look at some of the basic biblical truths about worship.

One of the Hebrew words translated "worship" means to bow down. Another Hebrew word translated "worship" means to serve. Biblical worship therefore covers both our adoration of God and the practical service we offer Him.

One of the ways that people worshipped God was by offering sacrifices to Him:

> Isaiah 19:21 (ESV)
> **21** And the LORD will make himself known to the Egyptians, and the Egyptians will know the LORD in that day and worship with sacrifice and offering...

In the New Testament, we no longer offer animal sacrifices to God, because the blood of Jesus has now been shed for us, which takes away our sin forever. However, we do still offer financial sacrifices to God by giving generously to the church so that she can fulfil her mission, be a source of charity to the poor, and support her ministers:

> Acts 4:34–35 (ESV)
> **34** There was not a needy person among them, for as many as were owners of lands or houses sold them and brought the proceeds of what was sold **35** and laid it at the apostles' feet, and it was distributed to each as any had need.

> 1 Timothy 5:16–18 (ESV)
> **16** If any believing woman has relatives who are widows, let her care for them. Let the church not be burdened, so that it may care for those who are truly widows.
> **17** Let the elders who rule well be considered worthy of double honor, especially those who labor in preaching and teaching. **18** For the Scripture says, "You shall not muzzle an ox when it treads out the grain," and, "The laborer deserves his wages."

> Hebrews 13:16 (ESV)
> **16** Do not neglect to do good and to share what you have, for such sacrifices are pleasing to God.

> Philippians 4:16–18 (ESV)
> **18** ... I am well supplied, having received from Epaphroditus the gifts you [i.e. the Philippian church] sent, a fragrant offering, a sacrifice acceptable and pleasing to God.

We also offer God the sacrifice of praise as part of our worship:

Hebrews 13:15 (ESV)
¹⁵ Through him then let us continually offer up a sacrifice of praise to God, that is, the fruit of lips that acknowledge his name.

As we offer to God the sacrifice of praise, there are various physical expressions that may accompany it. Such expressions include...

1. Singing:

> Psalm 100:2 (ESV)
> ² Serve the LORD with gladness!
> Come into his presence with singing!

2. Dancing:

> Psalm 149:3 (ESV)
> ³ Let them praise his name with dancing,
> making melody to him with tambourine and lyre!

3. Clapping our hands

> Psalm 47:1 (ESV)
> ¹ Clap your hands, all peoples!
> Shout to God with loud songs of joy!

4. Joyful shouting:

> Psalm 66:1 (ESV)
> ¹ Shout for joy to God, all the earth;

5. Lifting our hands:

> Psalm 63:4 (ESV)
> ⁴ So I will bless you as long as I live;
> in your name I will lift up my hands.

6. Music:

> Psalm 33:2-3 (ESV)
> ² Give thanks to the LORD with the lyre;
> make melody to him with the harp of ten strings!
> ³ Sing to him a new song;
> play skillfully on the strings, with loud shouts.

God dwells in our praise in a special way. As we praise God, we should therefore expect to encounter Him:

> Psalm 22:3 (KJV)
> ³ But thou *art* holy, *O thou* that inhabitest the praises of Israel.

Biblical worship also includes offering ourselves totally to God for Him to have His way in our lives:

> Romans 12:1-2 (ESV)
> I appeal to you therefore, brothers, by the mercies of God, to present your bodies as a living sacrifice, holy and acceptable to God, which is your spiritual worship. ²Do not be conformed to this world, but be transformed by the renewal of your mind, that by testing you may discern what is the will of God, what is good and acceptable and perfect.

John 4:24 (ESV)
[24] God is spirit, and those who worship him must worship in spirit and truth."

14

Death

In this chapter, we will explore what happens when we die.

Because of sin, death is inevitable for all human beings:

> Romans 6:23 (ESV)
> [23] For the wages of sin is death, but the free gift of God is eternal life in Christ Jesus our Lord.

> Hebrews 9:27 (ESV)
> [27] And just as it is appointed for man to die once, and after that comes judgment,

After death, the body begins to decompose. But what happens to the immaterial part of man (the spirit and soul) when he dies?

Before Christ ascended back to heaven, all people, whether righteous or unrighteous, went to a place that is called Sheol in the original Hebrew language of the Old Testament. For example, Jacob and the psalmist anticipated going there when they died:

> Genesis 42:38 (ESV)
> **38** But he said, "My son shall not go down with you, for his brother is dead, and he is the only one left. If harm should happen to him on the journey that you are to make, you would bring down my gray hairs with sorrow to Sheol."

> Psalm 88:3 (ESV)
> **3** For my soul is full of troubles,
> and my life draws near to Sheol.

The wicked also went to Sheol:

> Psalm 9:17 (ESV)
> **17** The wicked shall return to Sheol,
> all the nations that forget God.

The equivalent word for Sheol in Greek is "Hades". This is clear from the fact that when Psalm 16:10 is quoted in the New Testament (which was written in Greek), the word "Hades" is used in place of Sheol:

> Psalm 16:10 (ESV)
> **10** For you will not abandon my soul to Sheol,
> or let your holy one see corruption.

> Acts 2:27 (ESV)
> **27** For you will not abandon my soul to Hades,
> or let your Holy One see corruption.

The Bible reveals that there are various compartments in

Hades (more than I will mention here). At death, the righteous went to a compartment where the patriarch Abraham was, and the wicked went to a different compartment in which they were tormented.

> Luke 16:19-26 (ESV)
> [19] "There was a rich man who was clothed in purple and fine linen and who feasted sumptuously every day. [20] And at his gate was laid a poor man named Lazarus, covered with sores, [21] who desired to be fed with what fell from the rich man's table. Moreover, even the dogs came and licked his sores. [22] The poor man died and was carried by the angels to Abraham's side. The rich man also died and was buried, [23] and in Hades, being in torment, he lifted up his eyes and saw Abraham far off and Lazarus at his side. [24] And he called out, 'Father Abraham, have mercy on me, and send Lazarus to dip the end of his finger in water and cool my tongue, for I am in anguish in this flame.' [25] But Abraham said, 'Child, remember that you in your lifetime received your good things, and Lazarus in like manner bad things; but now he is comforted here, and you are in anguish. [26] And besides all this, between us and you a great chasm has been fixed, in order that those who would pass from here to you may not be able, and none may cross from there to us.'

When Jesus ascended to heaven, it seems that He took with Him all the righteous who were with Abraham. That is how some interpret Ephesians 4:8:

> Ephesians 4:8 (ESV)
> [8] Therefore it says,

"When he [Jesus] ascended on high he led a host of captives,
and he gave gifts to men."

Today, now that Jesus died for our sins and has gone back to heaven; when believers die, we go straight to heaven to be with Christ. We no longer go to Hades:

> 2 Corinthians 5:8 (ESV)
> [8] Yes, we are of good courage, and we would rather be away from the body and at home with the Lord.

However, the unrighteous, like the rich man in Luke 16:19-26, still go to Hades when they die. They are there waiting for the day of judgment. When the day of judgment comes, then the bodies of all who are in Hades will be resurrected and reunited with their soul and spirit, and then their whole being will be thrown into yet another place called "the lake of fire". Hades and death itself will also be thrown there too (death will be destroyed forever):

> Revelation 20:11-15 (ESV)
> [11] Then I saw a great white throne and him who was seated on it. From his presence earth and sky fled away, and no place was found for them. [12] And I saw the dead, great and small, standing before the throne, and books were opened. Then another book was opened, which is the book of life. And the dead were judged by what was written in the books, according to what they had done. [13] And the sea gave up the dead who were in it, Death and Hades gave up the dead who were in them, and they were judged, each one of them, according to

what they had done. **¹⁴** Then Death and Hades were thrown into the lake of fire. This is the second death, the lake of fire. **¹⁵** And if anyone's name was not found written in the book of life, he was thrown into the lake of fire.

Jesus referred to this final lake of fire as "gehenna" in the original language (often translated "hell"):

Matthew 10:28 (YLT)
²⁸ 'And be not afraid of those killing the body, and are not able to kill the soul, but fear rather Him who is able both soul and body to destroy in gehenna.

Mark 9:43-44 (YLT)
⁴³'... it is better for thee maimed to enter into the life, than having the two hands, to go away to the gehenna, to the fire—the unquenchable— ⁴⁴where their worm is not dying, and the fire is not being quenched.

When we die, though our body is dead, our soul is conscious. This is evident in that both Lazarus and the rich man were very conscious of what was going on when they were dead. John also clearly saw the souls of martyrs as very much alive and conscious in his vision:

Revelation 6:9-10 (ESV)
⁹ When he opened the fifth seal, I saw under the altar the souls of those who had been slain for the word of God and for the witness they had borne. ¹⁰ They cried out with a loud voice, "O Sovereign Lord, holy and true, how long before you will

judge and avenge our blood on those who dwell on the earth?"

There are some who wrongly teach that at death, the soul "sleeps" and is not conscious. However, when the Bible speaks of the dead sleeping, it is a reference only to the body. The body is described as sleeping because it will one day be awoken at the resurrection. That it is the body, and not the spirit / soul that sleeps at death is made evident in the following passage about the martyr Stephen:

> Acts 7:59-60 (ESV)
> [59] And as they were stoning Stephen, he called out, "Lord Jesus, receive my spirit." [60] And falling to his knees he cried out with a loud voice, "Lord, do not hold this sin against them." And when he had said this, he fell asleep.

Stephen asked Jesus to receive his spirit. When his spirit left his body, his body then "fell asleep". When Jesus returns, Stephen's body will be awakened and reunited with his spirit (which is now with Jesus):

> 1 Thessalonians 4:13-18 (ESV)
> [13] But we do not want you to be uninformed, brothers, about those who are asleep, that you may not grieve as others do who have no hope. [14] For since we believe that Jesus died and rose again, even so, through Jesus, God will bring with him those who have fallen asleep. [15] For this we declare to you by a word from the Lord, that we who are alive, who are left until the coming of the Lord, will not precede those who have fallen asleep.

16 For the Lord himself will descend from heaven with a cry of command, with the voice of an archangel, and with the sound of the trumpet of God. And the dead in Christ will rise first. **17** Then we who are alive, who are left, will be caught up together with them in the clouds to meet the Lord in the air, and so we will always be with the Lord. **18** Therefore encourage one another with these words.

Because Jesus has conquered death, when those who have believed in Him are resurrected, their bodies will be immortal, just like Jesus' body:

1 Corinthians 15:42 (ESV)
42 So is it with the resurrection of the dead. What is sown is perishable; what is raised is imperishable.

15

The Second Coming of Jesus Christ

In this final chapter, we look at the basic biblical truths about Christ's second coming.

Jesus Christ returned to heaven, but He is coming back again:

> Acts 1:10-11 (ESV)
> [10] And while they were gazing into heaven as he went, behold, two men stood by them in white robes, [11] and said, "Men of Galilee, why do you stand looking into heaven? This Jesus, who was taken up from you into heaven, will come in the same way as you saw him go into heaven."

Jesus has gone away to prepare a place for us in His Father's house (heaven). When He comes again, He will take us there:

> John 14:1-3 (ESV)
> "Let not your hearts be troubled. Believe in God;

believe also in me. ²In my Father's house are many rooms. If it were not so, would I have told you that I go to prepare a place for you? ³And if I go and prepare a place for you, I will come again and will take you to myself, that where I am you may be also.

No one, except God, knows when Christ will return:

Matthew 24:36 (ESV)
³⁶"But concerning that day and hour no one knows, not even the angels of heaven, nor the Son, but the Father only.

The church is to look forward to Christ's return. The bodies of dead believers will be resurrected and we who are still alive when He comes will be caught up to meet Him in the air. Our bodies will be gloriously transformed so that they are just like Jesus' body:

1 Thessalonians 4:15-17 (ESV)
¹⁵For this we declare to you by a word from the Lord, that we who are alive, who are left until the coming of the Lord, will not precede those who have fallen asleep. ¹⁶For the Lord himself will descend from heaven with a cry of command, with the voice of an archangel, and with the sound of the trumpet of God. And the dead in Christ will rise first. ¹⁷Then we who are alive, who are left, will be caught up together with them in the clouds to meet the Lord in the air, and so we will always be with the Lord.

Philippians 3:20-21 (ESV)
²⁰But our citizenship is in heaven, and from it we await a Savior, the Lord Jesus Christ, ²¹who will transform our lowly body to be like his glorious body, by the power that enables him even to subject all things to himself.

1 Corinthians 15:42-49 (ESV)
⁴²So is it with the resurrection of the dead. What is sown is perishable; what is raised is imperishable. ⁴³It is sown in dishonor; it is raised in glory. It is sown in weakness; it is raised in power. ⁴⁴It is sown a natural body; it is raised a spiritual body. If there is a natural body, there is also a spiritual body... ⁴⁹Just as we have borne the image of the man of dust, we shall also bear the image of the man of heaven.

When Christ comes, He will judge the living and the dead. The unrighteous dead will also be raised so that they can appear before Him for judgement and be thrown into the lake of fire:

2 Timothy 4:1 (NKJV)
I charge *you* therefore before God and the Lord Jesus Christ, who will judge the living and the dead at His appearing and His kingdom:

2 Corinthians 5:10 (ESV)
¹⁰For we must all appear before the judgment seat of Christ, so that each one may receive what is due for what he has done in the body, whether good or evil.

Romans 2:5–8 (ESV)

5 But because of your hard and impenitent heart you are storing up wrath for yourself on the day of wrath when God's righteous judgment will be revealed.

6 He will render to each one according to his works: **7** to those who by patience in well-doing seek for glory and honor and immortality, he will give eternal life; **8** but for those who are self-seeking and do not obey the truth, but obey unrighteousness, there will be wrath and fury.

Daniel 12:2 (ESV)

2 And many of those who sleep in the dust of the earth shall awake, some to everlasting life, and some to shame and everlasting contempt.

Revelation 20:11–15 (ESV)

11 Then I saw a great white throne and him who was seated on it. From his presence earth and sky fled away, and no place was found for them. **12** And I saw the dead, great and small, standing before the throne, and books were opened. Then another book was opened, which is the book of life. And the dead were judged by what was written in the books, according to what they had done. **13** And the sea gave up the dead who were in it, Death and Hades gave up the dead who were in them, and they were judged, each one of them, according to what they had done. **14** Then Death and Hades were thrown into the lake of fire. This is the second death, the lake of fire. **15** And if anyone's name was not found written in the book of life, he was thrown into the lake of fire.

The devil will be thrown into the lake of fire:

> Revelation 20:10 (ESV)
> [10] and the devil who had deceived them was thrown into the lake of fire and sulfur where the beast and the false prophet were, and they will be tormented day and night forever and ever.

The current earth and heavens, which have been corrupted by sin, will pass away. "Heavens" here is simply a reference to the sky (i.e. the space above where we see the clouds and stars e.g. "birds of the heavens" - Genesis 1:26). It is not to be confused with the spiritual heaven where God lives[1].

> Matthew 24:35 (ESV)
> [35] Heaven and earth will pass away...

> 2 Peter 3:10 (NKJV)
> [10] But the day of the Lord will come as a thief in the night, in which the heavens will pass away with a great noise, and the elements will melt with fervent heat; both the earth and the works that are in it will be burned up.

---

[1] Based on Revelation 20:1-6, some Christians believe that when Christ comes, He will rule with His people over the present earth for 1,000 years, and afterwards the earth and heavens pass away. However, other Christians interpret this passage symbolically and therefore do not believe in a literal 1,000 year reign after Christ returns. It is beyond the scope of this book to enter into this discussion, and so I have simply included the main aspects of this subject on which Christians generally agree.

We have seen that when Jesus comes, He will take us to the spiritual heaven to be with Him forever (John 14:1-3). But what will it be like there? It will look like a glorious new earth and new heavens (i.e. sky):

> 2 Peter 3:10-13 (NKJV)
> [10] But the day of the Lord will come as a thief in the night, in which the heavens will pass away with a great noise, and the elements will melt with fervent heat; both the earth and the works that are in it will be burned up. [11] Therefore, since all these things will be dissolved, what manner *of persons* ought you to be in holy conduct and godliness, [12] looking for and hastening the coming of the day of God, because of which the heavens will be dissolved, being on fire, and the elements will melt with fervent heat? [13] Nevertheless we, according to His promise, look for new heavens and a new earth in which righteousness dwells.

> Revelation 21:1 (ESV)
> Then I saw a new heaven and a new earth, for the first heaven and the first earth had passed away, and the sea was no more.

The heavenly Jerusalem, the city of God, will be there, in which will be the throne of God and of the Lord Jesus. We will be with God and His Son forever, and we will reign throughout eternity:

> Hebrews 12:22 (ESV)
> [22] But you have come to Mount Zion and to the city of the living God, the heavenly Jerusalem, and to innumerable angels in festal gathering,

Revelation 21:2-4 (ESV)

² And I saw the holy city, new Jerusalem, coming down out of heaven from God, prepared as a bride adorned for her husband. ³ And I heard a loud voice from the throne saying, "Behold, the dwelling place of God is with man. He will dwell with them, and they will be his people, and God himself will be with them as their God. ⁴ He will wipe away every tear from their eyes, and death shall be no more, neither shall there be mourning, nor crying, nor pain anymore, for the former things have passed away."

Revelation 21:9-11,22-23 (ESV)

⁹ Then came one of the seven angels who had the seven bowls full of the seven last plagues and spoke to me, saying, "Come, I will show you the Bride, the wife of the Lamb." ¹⁰ And he carried me away in the Spirit to a great, high mountain, and showed me the holy city Jerusalem coming down out of heaven from God, ¹¹ having the glory of God, its radiance like a most rare jewel, like a jasper, clear as crystal.

²² And I saw no temple in the city, for its temple is the Lord God the Almighty and the Lamb. ²³ And the city has no need of sun or moon to shine on it, for the glory of God gives it light, and its lamp is the Lamb.

Revelation 22:3-5 (ESV)

³ No longer will there be anything accursed, but the throne of God and of the Lamb will be in it [the new Jerusalem], and his servants will worship him.

⁴They will see his face, and his name will be on their foreheads. ⁵And night will be no more. They will need no light of lamp or sun, for the Lord God will be their light, and they will reign forever and ever.